CONTEMPORARY
SOUTHEAST ASIAN
ARTS and
CRAFTS

To the anonymous artists
and craftsmen of Southeast Asia
who have given us so much

CONTEMPORARY SOUTHEAST ASIAN ARTS and CRAFTS

ETHNIC CRAFTSMEN AT WORK
WITH HOW-TO INSTRUCTIONS FOR
ADAPTING THEIR CRAFTS

Thelma R. Newman

CROWN PUBLISHERS, INC.   NEW YORK

*Inquiries should be addressed to Crown Publishers, Inc.,
One Park Avenue, New York, N.Y. 10016.*

*Printed in the United States of America
Published simultaneously in Canada by
General Publishing Company Limited*

Designed by Manuela Paul

Library of Congress Cataloging in Publication Data
Newman, Thelma R
    Contemporary Southeast Asian arts and crafts.
    Bibliography: p.
    Includes index.
    1. Handicraft—Asia, Southeastern. I. Title.
TT113.S6N48   1976   745.5'095   76-13646
ISBN 0-517-52729-4
ISBN 0-517-52730-8 pbk.

CONTENTS

ACKNOWLEDGMENTS

Great debts of gratitude are owed to many people who extended extraordinary effort to help me. Among those in Indonesia are: Mrs. Louise D. Ansberry, whose knowledge of Indonesia is vast and who helped facilitate my travels there; Dr. Ibnu Sutowo, Managing Director of Pertamina, and Mrs. Annie J. Kalalo, Deputy Director of Tunas Indonesia, both of whom provided generous hospitality and guidance. In the Philippines: Mr. and Mrs. Roberto Reyes of Quezon City; Lorenzo J. Cruz, Director of the Bureau of National and Foreign Information, Manila; George Reyes of the Philippine Consulate. In Thailand: Mrs. Boonthien Ramdeja, Director of Narayana Phand in Bangkok, and Mr. Sirichai Saiphatama of Handicraft Promotion in Bangkok.

My deep appreciation also goes to Cecile Afable, editor and author, of Baguio; Dottie Anderson, Santa Cruz Mission, who shared some of her work in the Peace Corps with me; Angie N. Cruz of Zamboanga; Tony Enriquez, author, and Joy Enriquez, anthropologist, of Zamboanga; Martha Ibrahim, Mrs. Ansberry's secretary in Jakarta; Ms. H. Andi Muddariah, community leader and exponent of the silk industry in Sengkang; Dionisio G. Orellana, artist and expert on the arts of Mindanao; Mr. Felix V. Rosario of Zamboanga; Mrs. M. Soeharyo of Beng-Solo Trading Corp.; Attie Suliantoro Sulaiman of Jogjakarta; Nora Suryanti, Indonesian crafts expert and guide extraordinaire; Mrs. Tarntip Vichitslip of Chiang Mai.

Many thanks, as well, to José H. Alcid, Captain, Philippine Air Lines; Dr. Lydia Aznar-Alfonso of Cebu; Mayor Eulogio E. Borres of Cebu City; Mayor Camilo P. Cabili of Iligan City; Agnes Demetria, anthropologist, Zamboanga; Commander Tirso Dominguez of San Ramon; Eulogia C. Enriquez, crafts promotion, Cebu City; Mrs. Milly Ganda, crafts expert of Jakarta and Bali; Made Jastina and I. Ketut Gide Paramartha (Pram) Kisuma, of Bali Tunas Indonesia; Pan American Air lines; Anak Agung Gede Rai of the Bali Beach Hotel; Dr. Mauyag M. Tamano, President, Mindanao State University; Ayub M. Tedju of Sumba Tunas Indonesia; Mrs. Chupanth Vesamavibul, assistant manager of Narayana Phand, Bangkok, and Mrs. Ventana Helabi, her assistant.

Very much involved in helping me do my field research and assist in picture taking were my sons Jay Hartley and Lee Scott, with my husband, Jack, holding down the fort and continuing as my quartermaster general. To them, my unending gratitude and devotion.

Special thanks go to Norm Smith for superb photo processing, and to Pat Weidner, gal Saturday.

All photographs by the author or her sons Jay Hartley and Lee Scott, unless otherwise noted.

PREFACE

Studying and gathering material about the arts and crafts of Southeast Asia was one of the most rewarding and interesting undertakings I have ever had. There is so much diversity and richness in Southeast Asian tribal and village craft that one is stimulated and energized. Viable art forms are still flourishing in many places in Southeast Asia, even after so many centuries of practice. There was so much to learn. Yet so little of the processes of the arts and crafts had ever been recorded.

The privilege of sharing with you the fruits of three visits to Southeast Asia fulfills the promises I had given to these marvelous artist-craftsmen to communicate what they are doing. These people have heard for so long that they live in "have not" countries. Here was something they could share, to give to the "haves."

I don't know what these labels mean when viewing the significance of what I had seen firsthand. I do believe that the material values of peoples who project these labels should be reexamined. With so advanced and remarkable a heritage, with so many profound contributions to the knowledge and skills that we have taken for granted, we should certainly qualify our terms. What I have seen is that, where technological-industrial achievement has trespassed, all that is left of indigenous culture (what is not now extinct) is a vulgarization of former art styles. (This has been a direct contribution of industrial societies.) Because of the depreciated value of what they had, these people no longer live with their former dignity, which once was nourished by their past homogeneous life-styles, but have become displaced people in their own countries. Consumerism has permeated their patterns of culture, transforming or transpiring the beautiful products of their labor and love. Many forms of art and craft have disappeared or have been aesthetically

The author (*right*) talking to I. Gusti Nyoman Lempad, aged 118, of Bali, who is looking at a photograph taken of himself the year before.

depreciated because these works are no longer valued or in demand. In exchange, is commonplace junk.

In *Contemporary Southeast Asian Arts and Crafts,* there is no clear distinction between fine art and craft. Nor do the Southeast Asians see one. What they fashion and express is a part of their lives, whatever we label it.

Contained here is a record of people working in their milieu. It is a firsthand, on-site collection of art forms that still exist, with a bit of the lore and atmosphere included to enrich understanding and appreciation of what is being done. A few examples clearly demonstrate the assimilation of technology as form and process. A few are created, for the most part, for a marketplace of anonymous buyers. Although most works shown here still reside in the domain of tradition, some are successfully achieving a new vital and viable form integrating what has come before with the persistent images of today. Some of these contemporary works, no doubt, will become tomorrow's tradition continuing the evolutionary dimension of art.

With a new nationalism, leaders of these Southeast Asian countries should look to their potential resources in the arts and crafts, not only for enriching tourism or the export market but more importantly for reinforcing and expanding pride and self-concept and revaluing these rich traditions as a living art. Many of these forms are now cadavers of a past art that no longer has a place in people's lives but is relegated to museums.

In some areas, people were not amenable to the probings of a foreign author. War and revolt were in progress. In some places, we had to be escorted by armed guards. The material covered here, therefore, is by no means a complete survey but rather a representative sampling of Southeast Asian arts and crafts. Southeast Asia, geographically, is a large area covering about three

The photograph.

thousand miles from east to west and approximately two thousand miles from north to south. To describe every extant form and process would require several volumes of this size.

The author hopes that what you find here will go beyond providing information, and will inspire you to get into the process and try your hand at making some of these things. Perhaps what you see within will generate new ideas and keep alive in some small measure the richness of mankind's past achievements.

THELMA R. NEWMAN
February, 1976

TRANSMISSION
OF CULTURE
IN SOUTHEAST ASIA

There is a very different way of thinking about "art" in Southeast Asia. Art, in the Western sense of an aesthetic independent of anything else, does not exist. The Buddhist ethic is *oneness.* This permeates most Southeast Asian thinking about art. Everything is interrelated; everything is part of the whole, the one. Art is part of life and not a separate entity, in the same sense that religion is a part of life. It is a way to explain the universe.

The basis for this philosophy and aesthetic is avowedly religious. Religious law dictates how images may be portrayed. In the Hindu religion, man is not depicted in the natural, but rather in a stylized supernatural, symbolic manner. More so in the Moslem religion, where no image of man is described—not even abstractly; although in some cases some Hindu influence is seen, when Muhammad is depicted symbolically, as in the case of the Baruk of Mindanao, which transported Muhammad to Heaven.

Another crucial difference in conception is the evolutionary quality of form and design. Contemporary Southeast Asian art is the result of thousands of years of development. Old traditions are venerated; the new must prove themselves. Although styles have differed over the ages, motifs have remained consistent. Any variation was an extremely subtle expression of an artist or an age and was essentially a part of a whole body of cumulative effort and inspiration. The art maker was most often anonymous; the personal identity of the creator was usually sublimated to the greater meaning of a work. Radical new forms—which delight Western observers—are frequently viewed with indifference. Particularly in Hindu- and Buddhist-influenced art, every image is a copy, or a copy of a copy of a copy . . . of the legendary portraits of Buddha or of the Hindu gods. The artist is an agent of the universal soul rather than his own soul, as in the Western sense.

Old traditions are venerated. A ceremony awaited the author (*center*) upon crossing the threshold of H. Andi Muddariah's (*right of author*) house in Sengkang, Sulawesi. It started with a ceremonial bathing of the feet and ended with a feast and the traditional entertainment of dancing.

Art is a communication vehicle to describe, nonverbally, culture as a whole to the whole of culture. Art is not elitist. It speaks to everyone, rich and poor alike. Images are made to be worshiped; objects to be used. Form is the way something is made. Its purpose is its meaning.

In the West every last detail in traditional expression of subject matter is filled in and realistic depiction is considered a tour de force, whereas in the East there is generally an innate feeling for economy of line. Observers who, the Chinese realized, never see the same object in the same way fill in what is missing. Therefore symbols have even greater meaning when integrated with the observer's or worshiper's imagination.

There is a supranational linkup with the entire cultural area of Southeast Asia, with common cross-religious and cross-national characteristics. A vast iconographical system pervades, based on early common factors of migration and influences of two powerful, pervading forces in Asia—China and India. There are also great cultural differences as well. Some peoples of Southeast Asia are literate, others are nonliterate. Religions are diverse, and there are many different interpretations within the same basic religion. Regional customs are different. Environments are extremely varied and this influences which materials are used. Some social groups are tribal; other communities are more finely defined in a democratic social relationship familiar to some of the residents of the Western world.

Art and crafts are integrated into the lives of the Balinese.

Preparing decorative sweets for a ceremony in Bali. Four generations are involved.

Scarecrows made of bark cloth and bits of woven cloth are strung across the rice paddies of Luzon, in the Philippines, to frighten away birds. Making these—before rice ripens in the paddies—is a family affair among the Igorots.

Some people are nomadic, such as the Gadjaos (water gypsies), who live in boats on water all their lives and rarely step ashore. They ply the waters of southwest Mindanao, the Philippines, near Zamboanga, for its harvest of shells.

Some social groups, such as the North Thailand people called Akha, are tribal.

Communities are slowly coming under the influence of universals. This road, constructed to carry trucks and cars, is still plied by horse and wagon, bicycle and man-carried panniers. The scene is from Tempe, Sulawesi, Indonesia.

Environments have modified Moslem religious practice. Customs of the Buginese have been influenced by the Chinese as can be seen in their last remaining treasure from the past, displayed here by H. Andi Muddariah and her sister.

Although the art forms described in this book can still be seen in active use much as they have existed for centuries, there is a decrease in demand and, in some cases, a diffusion of intent. Technology has created the need for a new brand of art and craft for the marketplace. The craftperson, instead of making something for someone known, creates now for the ubiquitous tourist. The process is more impersonal. But the hand still is the primary motor, and the time it takes to create something is not yet a dominating consideration. Products continue to be made in homes and in small village shops using the same materials of the immediate environment, the essential traditions of design form and the same human energy as before. Work still preserves the mark of the craftperson, even though his or her presence is more indirect and the number of persons working in the arts and crafts is diminishing. There are now many extinct art forms. But that is as it always has been, though greatly accelerated in today's world. Society, its functions and products needed for the exercise of cultural patterns, is not static. Demands change. The problem is that new products are too much the same, as everywhere else in the world. The art forms are not evolving but being transformed by foreign influence. Technologically inspired products, with their pervading universality and aesthetic, are impoverishing the world. Art and craft, as communication, are becoming everywhere identical.

Old processes are modified to fulfill different needs—as arts and crafts for the marketplace. Young girls, here, are learning to make a popular design in lacquerware, almost as meticulously as they did in the past. From Thailand.

Of the many extinct art forms, the carved wooden bowl (Ifugao, northern Luzon, the Philippines) has been replaced almost completely with enamel or polyethylene containers.

DEFINING SOUTHEAST ASIA: GEOGRAPHY AND CULTURE

Both geography and culture define Southeast Asia. The area so described includes the modern nations of Burma, Laos, Thailand, Cambodia, Vietnam, Malaysia, the Philippines, all the Indonesian islands (Sumatra, Kalimantan, Sulawesi, Java, Bali), the Lesser Sunda Islands (Sumba, Flores, etc.), and a culturally similar northwestern portion of New Guinea called Irian Jaya.

The geographical connection is clear: the southeastern corner of the Asian landmass forms a natural pocket. Mountains create a natural division running down the spine of Indochina. And though that boundary did not exclude northern and western influences, their infusion was slower and subtler than would have been possible across a plain. Chinese influences are keenly sensed in the east, and Indian influences on the west of the mountains. But they blend into forms distinctly Southeast Asian, neither clashing nor overlapping completely. That area shares a climate and, through the centuries, it has shared a host of outside traders, visitors, and conquerors.

In the same sense, the islands to the south and east are an integral part of the continent. Sumatra, Java, and Kalimantan lie very near to the mainland —separated only by a shallow sea covering the Sudanese Shelf. The islands can only have been, as they are even now, steppingstones along a route of trade and exploration extending from China to Melanesia and Australia. Not only do the Java and Flores seas provide "inland" waterways conducive to trade and communication, but the islands themselves break the tides between the South China Sea and the Indian Ocean. The line of transmission is further supported by theories involving the deep ravine of water running lengthwise between Kalimantan and Sulawesi known as Wallace's line: animals to the west are similar to those found in Asia (tigers, elephants, rhinoceroses, water buffalo, and orangutans); on the islands east of Wallace's line, animals resemble those found on the Australian continent (marsupials, cassowaries, etc.).

PREHISTORIC GEOGRAPHY: ARCHEOLOGICAL EVIDENCES OF CULTURE TRANSMISSION

In the Paleolithic period (400,000–120,000 B.C.), during the day of the Java man, sea levels were lower. The contemporary islands of Indonesia were a single landmass, connected to the continent of Asia by the Sudanese Shelf. Products of any kind were scarce; the only tool extant was a single-edged ax. Evidence from the Upper Pleistocene period (120,000–20,000 B.C.) suggests further developments. Our species changed physically, indicating, in part, a migration from Europe and Australia. The life-style, however, remained essentially the same.

By the time the seas rose at the end of the Pleistocene period, however, forming present-day island groupings, the human species and its skills had developed significantly. Modern forms of mankind appeared and flourished throughout Southeast Asia: Australoids, Paleomelanesids, Veddas, Negritos.

Although customs may vary greatly from area to area of Southeast Asia, many people have ancestors in common. The Kalinga tribe, northern Luzon, the Philippines . . .

... the T'boli group, Lake Sebu, South Cotabato, Mindanao, the Philippines, as well as ...

... this Buginese lady from Sengkang, Sulawesi, Indonesia. Different patterns of change, different environmental influences, have generated differences in culture.

Rather than allowing themselves to be cut off by the sea, some of these peoples must have crafted rafts and canoes, since contact with the Malay Peninsula and Indochina was maintained.

Other groups, however, retreated into the dense jungle of Kalimantan, Sulawesi, and Mindanao, eliminating all contact with outside groups and cultures. They remained hunters and food gatherers—as some do to this day in the farther reaches of Mindanao.

With the beginnings of agriculture, in the early Neolithic period (2000 B.C.), archeologists have been able to piece together the first patterns of cultural transmission. That yams, taro, and rice—staples of this day—existed then in a stable form seems certain. But the quadrangular and round axes provide the real clues. The same shapes have been traced through China, Formosa, the Philippines, eastern Indonesia, and New Guinea (the round ax), and from Southern China through the Malay Peninsula to Sumatra, Java, and the Lesser Sunda Islands (the quadrangular ax). Beaten pottery, still made and used in some parts, dates back to Neolithic times too.

During the late Neolithic Age, monuments evolved that commemorated a more highly developed social and religious order. These were called Megalithic monuments—named for both period and culture. In fact, some Megalithic cultures still exist in Assam (Indochina), West Burma, the Indonesian

Rice paddies of Bali are similar to those in northern Luzon, the Philippines.

Stone statues of Batak ancestors, Samosir Island, Lake Toba, Sumatra, Indonesia.

Beaten pottery is still made in some parts of Sulawesi, Indonesia, and in Luzon, the Philippines, in the traditional way.

Sarcophagi and altars are megalithic monuments of the past on Samosir Island.

Stone carving is a prolific art in Bali.

islands of Nias, Flores, and Sumba, and among some of the Toradjas of Central Sulawesi. Stone statues of ancestors, sarcophagi, and altars of this period can be seen in Sumatra on Samosir Island in Lake Toba, as well as in Mindanao, Java, Sulawesi, and Bali. Examples of pottery engraved with geometric designs and sporting human faces have been uncovered as well.

 DESIGN INFLUENCES

Bronze and iron were introduced during the first millennium B.C. by the Dongson, a people who migrated eastward from an area that is now southern Russia to present-day Southern China/Northern Indochina. By the eighth century B.C., practically the whole of Thailand, Malaysia, and Indonesia was influenced by Dongson Culture. The Dongson were assimilated into the population and, in addition to bringing new materials and techniques, they brought new design influences. Bronze work, their chief product, was characterized by spirals, curvilinear figures, meanders, human figures facing frontward, trees of life, ships for dead souls. Those themes were metrical; they were repeated rhythmically, and the motifs spread from bronze objects to weavings and other craft forms. To this day, the Dongson influence can still be seen, particularly in Sumbanese textiles.

The Dongsons were bronze workers who brought their art and craft to Southeast Asia in the first millennium, B.C. The designs created by the people of Tugaya, Mindanao, the Philippines, are very much like those of their ancestors hundreds of years ago.

Note the design similarities of the bronze containers and this detail from a fabric woven in North Sumatra.

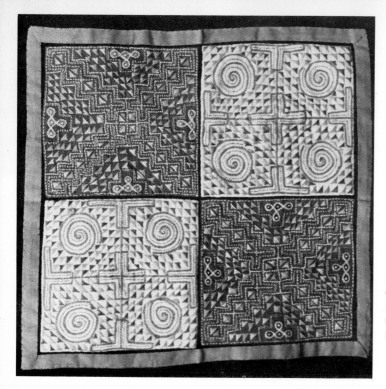

Further common design denominators in the embroideries of the Meo people of northern Thailand. Note that the spirals, scrolls, and repeat triangles (modified tumpal) are interpreted in all three examples.

China has a long history of assimilating nomadic tribes and embodying their skills and design motifs into its own art. Through such technical and aesthetic devices China, in turn, significantly influenced the art forms of the diverse cultures of the Pacific Basin—as far east as South America. The use of certain symbols: the lozenge, the long tongue, and monster headgear appear so persistently in other cultures that the possibility of simultaneous emergence is minimal. Some contacts are supported by documentary evidence, like the Siamese (Thai) imitations of Chinese Sung and Ming pottery —right down to the celadon glaze and identical shapes. In some parts of New Guinea, people treasure their ancient Chinese pottery. The Chinese also recorded other information about their southern neighbors and farther removed trading partners.

In 585 B.C., when the southern boundary of the Chinese empire was marked by the Yang-tze-Kiang River, Chinese historians wrote that barbarians inhabited the region below the river. Among those barbarians were the original Thai people, ancestors of the Siamese, Laotians, and Shans of today. The boundary, of course, was not as distinct as the Chinese scribe might have liked to believe. The Chinese and Thais along the river are cognate races that may have had a common link. Both their languages are similar in construction. It is interesting to note that customs of the hill-tribe people of northern Thailand, particularly the Yao, have much in common with the early customs of the peoples of southwestern China. Indeed, some groups had migrated to Thailand from China.

An ancient Chinese writer, Tan Chi Hu (twelfth century A.D.) wrote about a character by the name of Pien Hung who played a part in Chinese tales and myths of every Yao tribe. Tan Chi Hu claimed that Pien Hung was a barbarian who abducted a Chinese princess (circa 2400 B.C.). He took her to Hunan Province. According to legend, it was Pien Hung and the princess who parented the Yao.

Vase and stand, as well as floral arrangement, have been influenced by the Chinese. Attie Suliantoro Sulaiman of Jogjakarta, Java, Indonesia, created this arrangement.

A contemporary example of Chinese influence in a porcelain vase with indigo design, from Thailand.

The ubiquitous parasol. Made near Chiang Mai, Thailand.

Indian influence can be seen in the wats of Thailand.

K'ang Tai, from China, who headed a mission to Fu-nan (now Cambodia, Laos, Cochin China, Thailand, and part of Malaysia) circa A.D. 245–250, transmitted a description of some of the people of Fu-nan that appeared later in a history of the Tsin dynasty (A.D. 265–419). He spoke of walled cities with palaces and houses; and of men who were "ugly and black with curly hair." He described them as naked and barefooted and being an agrarian people; and that they were fond of engraving and chiseling ornaments. He spoke of eating utensils formed of silver and that taxes were paid in gold, silver, pearls, and perfumes. These people, according to K'ang Tai, also had books, archives, and an alphabet that resembled that of the Hou (a Central Asiatic tribe that had an Indian alphabet).

Other influences came from Indian cultures. Indeed, an Arab merchant called Sulayman (a common name in Indonesia today) in A.D. 851 had traveled in both India and China, Sumatra, and Java and wrote of the similarities of what he saw to the culture of the Dravidians who lived in southern India.

In the third century B.C., the epic Indian stories *Mahābhārata* and *Ramayana* proliferated throughout Southeast Asia and are to this day interpreted in paintings, sculptures, puppet and shadow plays, and dance, as well as literature. Cultural contacts and influences with India reached a high point with the construction of Angkor Wat, in Cambodia, and Hindu monuments in Java and Bali, but the greatest Indian influence came about through transmission of myths, ceremonial rites, and their instruments, peacefully, through trading and intermarriage. The Hindu-Javanese empire spread throughout Southeast Asia all the way to India. On the other hand, Chinese influence came with the colonizers and conquerors. The Chinese, Tibetans, Cambodians, and Thais were involved intermittently with wars and rebellions for centuries.

Neighboring countries influenced each other. In Thailand, the early Cambodians affected their culture in the southeast, the Burmans in the northeast, and the Malayans in the south. Even the Javanese influenced Thai culture, particularly in the early ninth century A.D. when the size of the Java empire was much larger than the perimeter of its present island.

Along a klong in Bangkok, Thailand, one has to look carefully for the automobile, the only evidence that the picture was taken recently. Otherwise, this scene (figuratively) could have dated back several hundred years.

A Buddhist temple of Thailand.

Islam came later, after Indian and Chinese influences established a long history of traditions. In Malaysia and Java, Hindu and Buddhist customs did not completely displace but frequently blended with the religious customs underlying Islam. Islam integrating with these cultures brought a new vitality and new ceremonial usages to the arts. In the Philippines, Islamic acculturation dominated only in the southern islands (beginning seventh or eighth century A.D.). The Malayan influence was also very strong. There are also strong affinities among the Islamic cultural forms of Mindanao, Philippines, with those of Sumatra, Nias, Sarawak, East Kalimantan, Sulawesi, and, as indicated earlier, Malaysia.

Despite Chinese and Indian influences in the pagan north of the Philippines, the mountain people still consist of seven ethnolinguistic groups who have maintained their separate identities, each with their own culture, ceremonial practices, and art traditions. (Most Philippine peoples are more or less homogeneous with the southern Mongoloid or Malayan peoples of Malaysia and Indonesia.) And although the Dutch brought cultural influences in the sixteenth century as traders, and the Spaniards came to annex territory in the south, followers of Islam more or less maintained their revisionist forms of worship, probably because Islam was more syncretic and tolerant of native practices. Today, different Moslem ethnic groups maintain an overall spiritual identity under Islamic brotherhood but do not necessarily share common and artistic characteristics, even within the same island, because of variations in the general practice of Muslims and in the acculturation of local customs.

A Yakan funeral.   *Photo Courtesy: Dottie Anderson*

Indigenous customs of a region blend with Islamic practice. At a funeral bier in Basilan, the Philippines, the Yakan people create arrangements with eggs—symbolizing whence they came . . .
Photo Courtesy: Dottie Anderson

Some forms change little from one area to another. These plaited ornaments are from Sulawesi, Indonesia.

A Yakan from Basilan, the Philippines, creates a plaited shape.
Photo Courtesy: Dottie Anderson

A young man in northern Thailand plaits ornamental forms.

 SOME UBIQUITOUS ART FORMS

It is fascinating to trace the transmission of art forms throughout the area. The kris is a sharp-bladed weapon symbolizing bird or snake or serpent motif, with a close connection between blade and serpent. In the Philippines, the owner or maker, in order to consecrate the kris, brings the blade into contact with the entrails or brain of a snake. Similar kris forms can be seen in virtually every country of Southeast Asia.

A T'boli man wearing abaca clothing and an important kris (knife in sheath). From Lake Sebu, South Cotabato, Mindanao, the Philippines.

Yakans of Basilan wearing kris. These kris can be found all over Indonesia as well.

The buffalo signifies fertility. This one lives in Sulawesi, Indonesia.

The buffalo's horns can be seen mounted on roof peaks from Batak (Sumatra), Dayak (Kalimantan), Maranao (the Philippines), to northern hill tribes (Thailand). This is a Batak house in Sumatra, Indonesia.

Another common symbol is that of buffalo horns mounted at the pointed top of a roof. As late as 1966 a young male buffalo was sacrificed annually by the Lawa in the center of the town to honor its founder, Meng Rai. Some claim that still happens today. Buffalo horns symbolized fertility and the bountiful earth. These horns could be seen in Chiang Rai Province in Lawa and Akha villages of Thailand, in northern Burma, in Assam, India, on Batak houses in Sumatra, Indonesia, in Buginese villages of Sulawesi, and in regions of Mindanao.

After a while, the initial reason or meaning for a design is lost, but vestiges remain, as in the rooftop of this Buginese house near Sengkang, Sulawesi, Indonesia. Only a part of the original buffalo horns are left.

Toko Mudaria of Bali, Indonesia, performing the betel nut ceremony.

The nagas of the past now reside in museums. This
naga is from Kuala Lumpur, Malaysia.

Chewing betel nut is also common throughout Southeast Asia, and there
are a host of containers designed to contain betel nut for storage and for
ceremony.

The naga, or mythical serpent or dragon, which has had both Indian and
Chinese origins, appears throughout in highly symbolic forms. Curiously, the
word "naga" means serpent in Sanskrit, but it is also the name of an ethnic
group of Assamese in northern India. (This is one place where the Dongson
settled.) The naga can be seen in various forms throughout Asia and Melanesia.

> Hence the trees change into shadows
> and the spirit of the ancestors
> animates the living world.
>
> *mpu* Tan Akung, twelfth century, in
> Kidung Wrtta Sançaya
> (from *Song of Kidung Madraka*)

2

TEXTILES–APPLIED DESIGN

 BACKGROUND

If the beauty and proliferation of remarkable textiles are any measure of a civilization, then the countries of Southeast Asia have attained a high order of cultural achievement. Notwithstanding remarkable weavings, batiks and embroideries are also significant and still function as the dominant clothing fabric for the regions where they are made.

Although a kind of batik originated in India, the highest form of batik, *tjanting batik,* developed in Java and on the island of Madura (situated to the north of Eastern Java). Two other kinds of batik making exist in Southeast Asia—stick batiking by the Toradjas of Central Sulawesi and starch paste batik found in West Java.

Tjanting batiking is a resist, or reserve, dyeing technique that dates back to the 1600s. The word itself, "batik," means "drawing" in Javanese. A small copper wax reservoir called a *tjanting,* fitted with one or two spouts like a miniature teakettle, and fixed to a bamboo handle, is used to deliver fine lines and dots of melted wax to finely woven cotton cloth (more rarely silk cloth). The wax preserves the color of the cloth. Successive waxings, dyeings, and removal of the wax from certain areas result in a variety of color.

The other reserve dyeing techniques, which use paste (starch) as a resist material and stick bamboo wax, permit less precise designs. These designs are the simplest types of batik and are used on coarse cotton cloth.

The very fine nature of the tjanting spout and the resulting fine lines and dots require finely spun, closely woven cotton or cambric cloth. These fabrics were not woven in Java and required importation at earliest stages of batik making from India and later through the Dutch and Japanese.

The Indian origin of batik was probably a type found in South India in which wax was applied with a stick and/or wooden stamping block. The

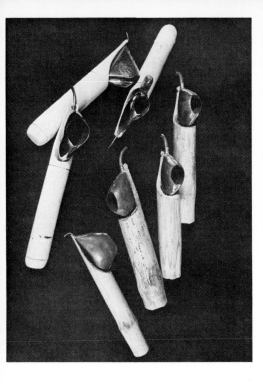

A mixture of waxes is melted in a pot over a low flame.

The finest Javanese batiks are drawn with finely tipped tjantings. Some come with double spouts. Usually the cuplike reservoir to hold wax is made of brass and the handle is bamboo.

earliest pieces extant, discovered in Java, were indeed printed on Indian handloomed cotton and sported Indian-type floral motifs. Because the tjanting is a Javanese invention, the style of batik became distinctively Javanese with only some of the early Hindu-Javanese idioms still flourishing.

It is a highly vital art that survived the collapse of Hindu rule in Java and the conversion of Java to Islam in the late sixteenth century, and competition from the printed cotton industry introduced by the Dutch in Djakarta (then known as Batavia). It still is Indonesia's most significant art form. And batik is still identified throughout the world with Java.

The *parang rusak* ("dagger point," or "broken blade") is a princely pattern once worn only by members of the royal house at Djakarta. This particular batik had been stamped with a tjap.

Now parang rusak is one of the most popular patterns; this one has a border. Note that the pattern is more irregular than the other example, indicating that the design was made with a tjanting.

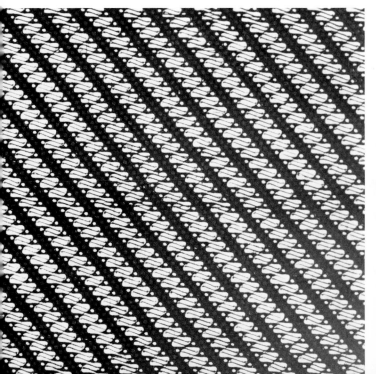

Tjanting batik, or batik tulis, originally was said to be a court art because it was a domestic occupation of female nobility. Certain patterns were reserved solely for court use. The two most traditional forms centered on the royal courts at Djakarta and Surakarta (Solo), both in Central Java. The *parang rusak* ("dagger point," or "broken blade") known as "Princely Pattern" was worn only by members of the royal house at Djakarta. And the *kawang,* consisting of an ancient Asiatic pattern traceable to the Mohenjodaro culture of the Indus Valley in India (second millennium B.C.), was another court design. Certain colors were indigenous as well—indigo and brown belonged to Central Java, while red and yellow occurred in northern and eastern sections.

Batiks are worn in Java (and Bali) by both sexes. Men wear headcloths, *kain kapala,* and shirtcloths, or sarongs, called *kain pandjang.* The kain kapala usually has a central motif and a design bordering its 3 1/2-foot square, while the kain pandjang, 3 1/2 by 8 1/2 to 10 feet, sports an overall pattern.

Batiks worn by women are breastcloths, *kemben,* shoulder scarfs called *slendang,* and skirtcloths, or *sarongs.* The scarf is 18 by 7 1/2 inches and sometimes, when longer, is used by dancers as sashes. Usually the slendang serves as a shopping bag or sling to carry children.

Since tjanting batik making is a slow process taking two weeks to two months to complete, a faster process was introduced in the middle of the nineteenth century. The *tjap,* a pair of copper blocks, is dipped into wax and

A very fine old *kain kapala,* or headcloth, which is worn by men.

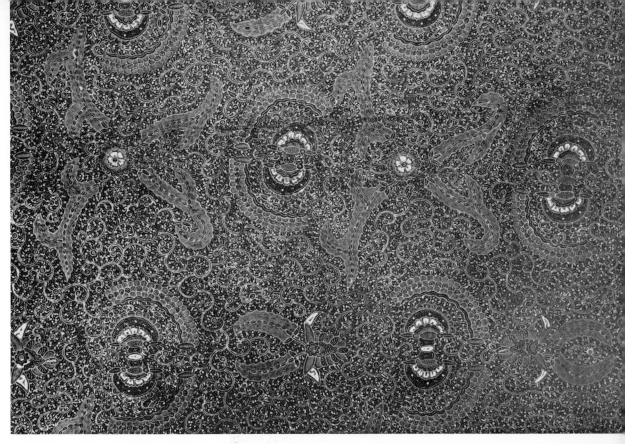

A traditional, very finely patterned sarong in white,
terra cotta, and indigo.

A close-up. Finely executed sarongs such as this
tjanting batik take at least three weeks to make.

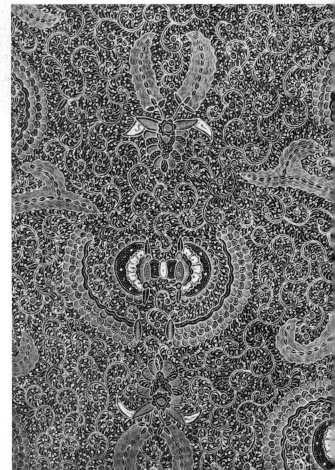

A closeup of the kain kapala showing the
tjanting-made design. Colors are traditional
—creamy white, beige, and indigo.

is then stamped on both sides of the cloth, speeding up the process. Whereas tjanting batik is woman's work, the tjap is used by men, who with this method produce up to twenty sarongs a day, compared to one piece taking fourteen days to two months. The stamped cloths, naturally, are not so valued as the true tjanting batik, even though the latter also takes a great deal of skill and closely resembles the former. Some designs employ both techniques, a compromise. An untrained eye often cannot tell the difference between the two processes. Essentially, the tjanting batik is more irregular in pattern and the tjap batik more regular and even. The dyeing, however, is still done by hand for both processes, and pieces subtly vary in color from batch to batch.

An interesting variation of the batik process is found in Bali. There the population was strongly influenced by Hindu-Javanese culture from the eleventh to the fourteenth century, but contact was cut off between the two areas after the fourteenth century when the Muslim states fought among themselves for control of Java. Since tjanting batik didn't emerge until the sixteenth and seventeenth centuries, the form of batik found in Bali is quite different and dates back to an earlier period. After stamping a paste resist on a fabric and then dyeing the background, the resist material is removed and glue is then stamped on the space left free of color. While the glue is still tacky, gold leaf is applied, producing a magnificent cloth used for ceremonial purposes, called *kain-prada.* Three highly stylized *tjeplokkan* (geometric type) motifs are superimposed on a geometrically divided background—a stylized lotus, a *bandji* motif (a basic design formed by a swastika and developed in geometric patterns, sometimes using flower and leaf symbols), and a *tumpal* (little triangles finishing off broader bands). The backgrounds are usually green or purple.

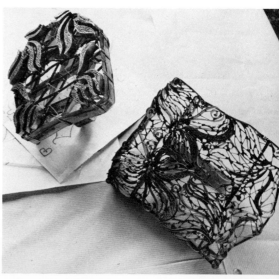

A tjap in process of being made. Copper is cut, shaped, and then soldered into a block to which a handle is attached.

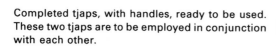

Completed tjaps, with handles, ready to be used. These two tjaps are to be employed in conjunction with each other.

A library of tjaps. The government of Indonesia considers these national treasures.

The tjap is dipped into hot wax that seeps through the cloth pad, which in turn is placed in the wax-melting pan . . .

. . . and is quickly pressed onto the cloth.

Sometimes the tjap is applied in a pattern.

Other times the design requires several co-ordinated tjaps, as shown here in a second application of wax.

THE TRADITIONAL BATIK PROCESS

The Preparation Process

STARCHING

Before any printing, fine white cotton cloth (cambric) is washed in clear water to remove the original starch. Then the cloth is restarched. Too heavy a starching will prevent the wax from sticking to the cloth. Too thin an application will cause the wax to penetrate the fibers too tenaciously, making removal difficult. A solution of rice water is used for starch. Starching prevents the cotton threads from distorting during the waxing process.

POUNDING (NGEMPLONG)

This pounding (ngemplong) process is used only for first-class tjanting batik. By pounding the cloth on a long board with a heavy wooden mallet, the cloth becomes supple and smooth. Finer drawing with the tjanting is then possible because the fabric is smoother.

Some designs are executed freely, by at first drawing a design on the finely woven cotton cloth.

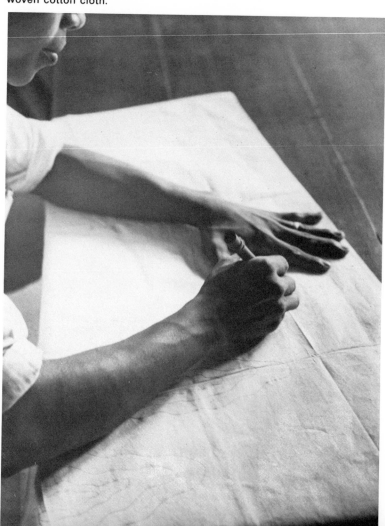

Then a craftsperson applies the melted wax with tjanting by dipping the tjanting into a pot that contains the wax . . .

. . . blowing congealed wax from the fine tip of the tjanting.

The Waxing Process

FIRST APPLICATION OF WAX (NGLOWONG)

After the fabric has been prepared, the batik process begins in the first of seven stages. In the first application of wax, the liquefied wax is drawn, or stamped, as the case may be, on both sides of the fabric. When the design is applied on one side, it is then repeated in reverse on the other side.

The wax formula for the first waxing using a tjanting is as follows:

2 parts resin	1 1/2 parts beeswax
1/2 part damar resin	1/5 part tallow (fat)
1/2 part paraffin	2 parts used wax

Banana leaves cover, pad, and insulate the table against heat of the wax for stamping with a tjap. This is the wax formula for the first tjap waxing:

4 parts resin	6 parts paraffin
1/2 part microcrystalline wax	1/2 part tallow

THE SECOND APPLICATION OF WAX

Prior to the dyeing process, the parts of the batik that are to remain uncolored should be thickly covered with wax on both sides of the cloth. This is called *nembok* or "wall," since the thick application of wax forms a barrier against the dye. If the wax wall is not thick enough, the dye will run through to the wrong parts of the batik, ruining the design. For that reason there is a different formula for this second application of wax. It is more sticky and flexible so that it does not crack when the cloth is lowered into the dyeing vats.

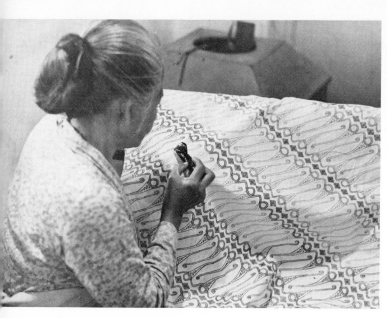

The wax is drawn on both sides of the cloth. Note that the lighter colored lines indicate that this is the other side of the fabric.

A close-up showing how the tjanting is held

In this nontraditional design, invention occurs as the batiker works.

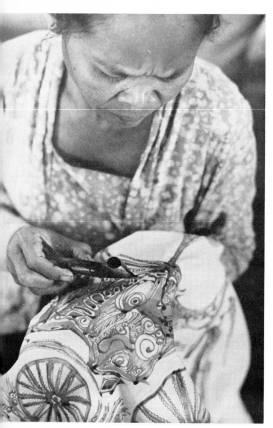

A group of women executing Bambang Oetoro designs.

This is the formula for the second or nembok application of wax when using a tjanting:

1 part resin   1/10 part tallow
1/2 part damar resin   1 part used wax
2/5 parts microcrystalline   1/10 part beeswax—preferably
   wax   from "baby" bees

The second application waxing formula when employing the tjap is as follows:

1 part resin   1/10 part tallow
3/10 part damar resin   1/6 part beeswax
1/10 part paraffin

The First Stage of Dyeing

The first steeping into dyestuff imparts a dark blue color. Before the advent of man-made dyestuffs, vegetable dyes, such as indigo and tree bark, were used and the process took days. After the cold dyestuff bath is mixed, the batik cloth is steeped until the desired color is achieved, and then the batik is hung up to dry in a shady spot. (Hot dyes would melt the wax.) The various dyes used today are naphthol As (Hoechst), Naphtazol (Francolor), Brenthol (ICI), Napthol (ACNA), Cibanaphtol (Ciba), Irganaphtol (Geigy), and Naphtanil (Du Pont). Each company has a different trade name for its dyes, which are petroleum by-products. Generally, the formula for these dyes is:

2 grams of dye
6 grams of salt
per each liter of water.

The batik being processed in a dye bath. In this instance, the fabric is rolled and unrolled into the vat.

In this case, the waxed fabric is dipped into the dye bath.

Wax Removal

When the required shade of blue has been obtained, the (first) layer of wax, parts that are to be dyed a brown color, is then scraped off with a dull knife, on both sides of the fabric. The second application of wax remains.

Unwanted wax is scraped off with a dull-bladed knife.

The Third Application of Wax

Then the blue that is to remain blue is waxed, while the parts to be dyed brown are left unwaxed. The wax is applied to both sides of the cloth. Some of the blue, when mixed with brown, will become a very dark, navy blue.

A third application of wax is applied to areas that are to remain blue.

Here a brush is used to apply wax to large areas.

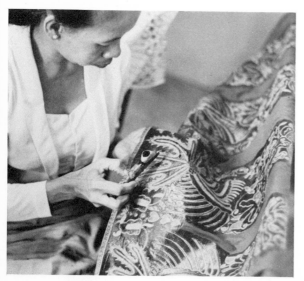

The Second Steeping

In the days when vegetable dyes were used, soga, a special kind of wood, was used to create the brown color. After each steeping, in those days, the cloth was allowed to dry overnight before it was again steeped in the soga to achieve the proper color. Chemical dyes require only a single steeping, which rarely takes longer than a half hour. *Lerak* is a soapy fruit that is used to wash the batik.

A second steeping in a brown dye bath is being applied.

Wax is removed from the fabric for the last time by soaking the waxed cloth in hot water until the wax runs off. (The wax is reclaimed by skimming after the water cools.)

The fabric is hung to dry on bamboo rods.

Removal of Wax

The cloth has now been dyed dark blue and brown. The wax is removed for the last time, this time by soaking the batik in boiling water until all the wax runs off. The fabric is hung to dry and is ready to be used. When the water cools, the wax is skimmed off and used in the formula that calls for "used wax."

HERE IS A RUNDOWN OF STEPS:

a. The first and second applications of wax.

b. The first dye bath (green) and a third application of wax.

c. Third application of wax is removed and the color area to be preserved is coated with wax and the piece is dyed indigo.

d. The wax is removed.

e. The border and a few spots are now protected with wax.

f. The piece is dyed beige; the wax is removed to reveal the finished design in indigo blue, green, beige, and a few specks of white.

A Garuda design in a traditional tjanting batik.

This batik from Tjirebon (Cirebon), Java, has a Chinese-influenced design and colors that are brighter than the indigos and browns of central and southern Java. This one is the famous cloud design called "Megamendung" in graded blues against a red background.

Adaptation of the Batik Process

Shortening the process only results in cruder products, although these shortcuts can be used to create very different design and color effects.

Bambang Oetoro creates contemporary batik paintings. Here is a cloth mounted vertically on a frame using spring clips.

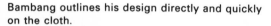

Bambang outlines his design directly and quickly on the cloth.

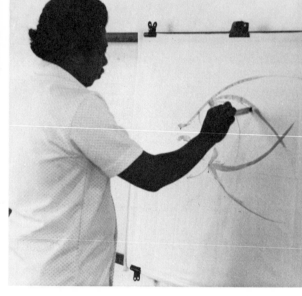

And follows up the broad outlines with more finely defined lines that are characteristic of the tjanting.

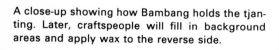

A close-up showing how Bambang holds the tjanting. Later, craftspeople will fill in background areas and apply wax to the reverse side.

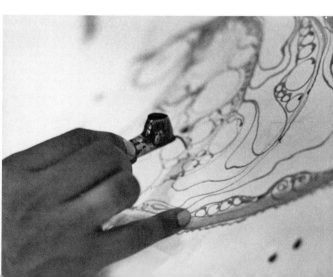

"Dragon" by Bambang Oetoro of Jogjakarta, Java.

A close-up showing detail and the characteristic crackle effect of batik. Black and blue symbolize long life, white signifies purity, and brown indicates power.

"Borobudur" by Bambang Oetoro.

A very large contemporary batik hanging (large enough to cover a king-sized bed) by Harry Soeharyo of Solo, Java.

MATERIAL AND EQUIPMENT

The traditional formula used by the Javanese is applicable for fine batik work. If all the ingredients are not available, try mixing pure beeswax with a little resin. For a crackle effect, use two-thirds paraffin and one-third beeswax. Microcrystalline waxes can be used with beeswax. Their flexibility, however, will not permit a crackle effect.

The tjanting can be purchased from some art material suppliers. If you find it difficult to obtain a tjanting, do as the Japanese—use a Japanese brush instead.

A frame is a good idea for stretching the fabric. An embroidery or a quilting frame is quite useful.

Use a small, deep saucepan for keeping the wax melted, or a No. 2 1/2 tin can and an electric hot plate. If you can afford it, an electric frying pan or a crockpot is an excellent container because you can regulate the wax temperature safely and there is no exposed heat source to cause a fire.

Large enamel or polyethylene containers are necessary for dyeing. Cold water dyes are excellent.

Fabric should be finely textured cotton or silk.

DIRECTIONS

Wash, starch (light mixture of liquid starch), and iron the fabric. Stretch the material tightly over a frame. Cover the table with layers of newspaper. Trace designs on the cloth lightly with a pencil or paint them on freehand with wax.

Melt the wax. If the wax smokes, it is too hot. Excessively hot wax runs out of control on the fabric; when too cool, it doesn't penetrate and piles up unnecessarily.

Apply wax to all parts of the design you wish to maintain the color of the cloth (on both sides).

Wet out the fabric with water and then dip it into the dye. Steep the fabric in the dye ten to thirty minutes, until the proper intensity is achieved. Remember that, when dry, the color will be lighter. Keep the dye bath agitated for more even dispersion of dye. Uneven dyeing can result from too strong a dye, too small a container, and not enough stirring. Most dyes adhere to fabric fibers better if they are as warm as possible. Wax resists can withstand heat up to about 110°F. Shake off excess dye so that color does not accumulate at the bottom, causing a darker color to collect there.

After dyeing, rinse the fabric in fresh water and allow it to dry in a shady spot.

Wax in, on both sides, areas to remain the newly dyed color and dye the cloth with a second color. Repeat the process as many times as needed. Remember that colors mix when dyed, too. So start with lightest colors and work to the darkest ones. Mixing complements together (red and green, yellow and purple, blue and orange) will produce degrees of gray to brown —sometimes with not too attractive effects.

Finally, to remove all the wax, place the batik in hot water. Keep the fabric agitated until all the wax has melted off. (Wax can be skimmed off when the water cools and can be reused.)

One can short-cut the dyeing process by brushing on dye in specific areas.

This is a contemporary Indian example of a very old process—tie and dye—which was thought to have originated in India. The rainbow cloth of Gianjar, Bali, appears to have been inspired by designs such as this.

Then, if a mordant is necessary (some dyes have mordants mixed into the dye mixture), use the mordant now. A bit of soap, salt, vinegar, or alum in the water can help to stabilize the dye. Make certain, too, that the dye is fast when hot water is used.

If different color dyes are to be used within wax-outlined areas, these different color dyes can be painted in the area with a brush. This method certainly can cut down the amount of work needed for multicolor effects.

Tie Dye, or Plangi

Tie and *dye,* or *plangi,* is another resist-dyeing process using tied-off or knotted areas of fabric to resist the penetration of dye. *Plangi* is a Malay term commonly used to describe the tying technique as distinguished from *trikit,* which is done by folding or gathering fabric together in patterns by stitching. The folds or gathers are held tightly by stitches that resist the absorption of dyes.

The earliest records of tie and dye date back to the sixth or seventh century. Marco Polo observed tie dyes in the caravansaries of China and India in the thirteenth century. Many of these fabrics were dyed with indigo (blue) or madder (red). They were striking and simple. In India the tied and dyed cloth was known as "bhandana work" from the Hindu verb *bhanda* meaning to tie. (The bandana of today is a derivation of this form.)

Tie and dye has appeared all over Asia—China, Thailand, Cambodia, Indonesia, and Mindanao in the Philippines. The work shown here is from Gianjar, Bali. One technique is called "rainbow cloth," a rough approximation of the very complex and fine tie and dye that existed in the past. Rainbow cloth is used in Bali as a sash around a woman's waist.

Another variation is a derivation designed for tourists and the young of today. Tomorrow, the adaptable tie and dye will be interpreted in yet another way.

THE PROCESS

The best material to use for tie and dye work is a lightweight fabric such as silk, rayon, or a fine cotton. The fabric is washed to remove fillers and then ironed. The design is then plotted on the cloth by means of tailor's chalk, pencil, pins, or with running stitches.

The way an area of fabric is gathered or folded, the angle and number of times a particular area is folded, will determine the pattern. The amount of tying and the type of tying material—how much and how tightly—will help determine how well folded areas will resist dyeing. Then the length of time the fabric is steeped in dye will also influence the degree of dye penetration.

After folding or gathering the specific spots to be tied, the area is wrapped tightly with a waxed thread or cord or polyethylene strips (used for tying packages) as the Balinese do. A 12-ply waxed cotton cord is good, so is button and carpet thread.

Then the dye bath should be prepared. Enamel pans, a hot plate for heating the dye, a wooden dowel for lifting and pushing the fabric around in the dye bath, and rubber gloves are essentials.

Dissolve the dye thoroughly in hot water; then add cold water to dilute the dye to the proper intensity and color. Try to maintain a temperature of about 104°F. (40°C.). Wet out the fabric for a few minutes in clear water before placing the fabric in a dye bath. Leave the fabric in the dye for the shortest time possible. The more intricate the work, the shorter the dyeing time should be. Squeeze out excess dye. If mordanting is necessary, this should have been done before the entire design process and any dyeing. This is called "bottom mordanting" and is used particularly for tie and dye and batik. The Balinese use aniline dyes and dip the fabric into naphthol for fixing it.

Rinse the fabric thoroughly after dyeing. Do not unwind strings until the fabric is almost dry. Then remove the strings, unfold the areas, and press while the fabric is slightly damp.

38

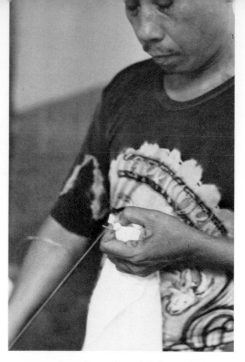

The rainbow cloth of Gianjar, Bali, is made by tieing off areas with plastic (polyethylene) string . . .

. . . wrapping the string tightly around and around and then fixing it with a slipknot.

The tied fabric is then steeped in dye . . .

. . . and rinsed in naphthol to fix the color.

Here the tied pieces are drying.

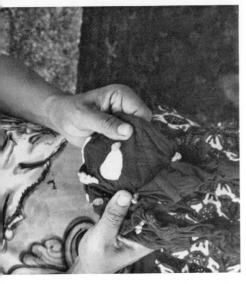

When dry, the string is removed, revealing an undyed shape.

Using a cotton swab, dye is painted within each shape, usually in different bright colors.

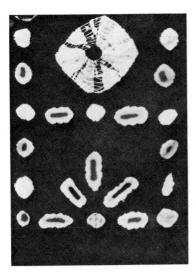

Two examples of different patterns in close-up.

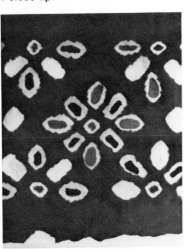

A completed cloth, which is used as a sash.

A Balinese woman in batik sarong and wearing a rainbow cloth around her waist, on her way to a temple to make an offering.

VARIATIONS

It is also possible to achieve different effects by tying the fabric into knots; tying an accordion-folded length of fabric at intervals; placing a pebble, button, or other object in an area and tying it; twisting the fabric instead of folding it; and as in trikit, folding and then sewing areas into gathers. The Balinese hand-paint areas or dip fabric into colors in order to increase the range of color and shorten the dyeing time. Disposable cotton swabs are employed for painting on colors. Batik and tie and dye can be combined as well.

A drawing of the Rangda is adapted for a tee shirt. The design is drawn directly on the shirt.

A variation on a theme, adapting ancient practice to contemporary format. Here cotton batting is wrapped around a stick to form a swab.

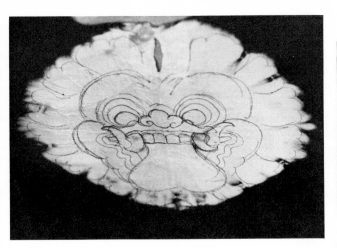

Using different swabs and many colors
of dye, Rangda emerges.

Shirts are left to dry and soon will be sold to tourists.

Embroidery and Appliqué

Embroidery numbers among the universal crafts, found all over the world. Both the people of China and India claim to have originated the embroidery arts—the Chinese as far back as 3000 B.C. Certainly the finest embroidery in the world today still comes from those areas. At one time a Chinese girl's marriageability depended upon her embroidery prowess. Indeed, many of the hill-tribe people of northern Thailand and Laos still maintain that custom.

Often embroideries contained precious stones, mirrors, seeds, beads, mica, shells, and precious metal-wrapped threads. Some of the most striking embroidered and appliquéd fabrics come from the Lampong district of South Sumatra. They combine their embroidery with a preplanned weaving, using, most often, bands of geometric elements repeated with some variations in progression up and down the cloth (for sarongs).

Two of the most common stitches are the cross-stitch and satin stitch. Yet an infinite variety of designs has emerged over the centuries. One group of people, the Yao, who are hill-tribe people of northern Thailand, have, since their flight from Szechwan, Hunan, Kiangsi, and Kweichow (and then to Kwangtung, Kwangsi, and Yunnan), China, in the fourteenth century, carried their culture principally by expressing it through embroidery on clothing. They now live in Tonkin, Laos, Burma, and northern Thailand. Legends and spirits adorned, protected, and transported the Yao in memory and time, preserving and identifying who and what they were. Abstract geometric embroidery symbolized their ancient story and their worship of nature's creations: the spirits of thunder, fire, flowers, animals, water, and mountains. And, for emphasis, legend is sometimes punctuated in formal tribal ceremony.

Long ago this embroidery once was worn on a Chinese empress's skirt. It is typical of the embroidery and appliqué techniq that influenced the people of Southeast Asia.

Over two thousand years of history are described with only about fifty needlework patterns, all executed with the cross-stitch. Yet their embroidery miraculously continues to be dynamic, alive, and vital. Although symbols may be copied from generation to generation, color and patterns are recombined into infinitely varied and complex designs. Skill and originality are requisites and a measure of a young girl's individuality and talent. She practices from the age of five or six until her betrothal and learns to master the vocabulary of all traditional designs. The maiden's geometric statement tells much about her view of nature, the spirit world, love, honor, daily life, and old legends to those sensitized to the symbolic language of her art. Her embroidered trousers, paradoxically, are at once traditional art and an art not required to be bound by tradition. More than that, the skill, knowledge, and sense of design that her work reveals will help her win a husband. Through her apprenticeship the Yao maiden is taught to synthesize every aspect of her life in embroidery. She knows that there is male and female, heaven and earth, light and darkness in everything. (Sun and light are male, moon and dark are female.) The Star Design, for example, signified all those Yao men who, at initiation into manhood, are assigned a guardian star to light their paths for the rest of their lives. Stars are ancestor spirits that have reached the Heavens and look after their earthly progenitors.

Before being assigned a guiding star, children are believed to be spirits of flowers. (*Waa* is a Yao word meaning both "flower" and "to be young.") Flower child spirits are playful and precious. A baby may wear no other clothing but his ubiquitous hat decorated with pompons, beads, shells, embroidery, and, sometimes, bells. Indeed a child looks like a flower gone mobile.

> "I've embroidered
> The lovers' embrace design.
> The lien pieng flowers
> Have already lost their fragrance
> I still wonder to myself
> Whose embrace are they . . ."

In a "Song of the Yao Maiden" (translated by Richard A. Kierstead), a young girl sings about her emerging womanhood in the fading fragrance of flowers, symbols of her childhood. She talks about depicting in embroidery this aspect of her life.

Through her apprenticeship, a Yao maiden is taught to synthesize every aspect of her life in embroidery. This Yao woman lives in the hills of northern Thailand.

She is working on a star design that symbolizes ancestor spirits that have reached the heavens.

Children, when very young, are believed to be spirits of flowers. A baby may wear no other clothing but this hat. Silver ornaments and chain, embroidery and pompons, make for a most elegant hat.

The Yao share much of their history with the Meo people, who are neighbors with a culture that also had originated in China. (They had migrated from the provinces of Kweichow and Hunan to Yunnan and Kwangsi and now live in Tonkin, Laos, Burma, and Thailand.) Sometimes designs are shared. The Meo also incorporate appliqué and batik patterns with their fabric decoration.

Another group of skilled embroiderers are the Karens, who are of Tibeto-Burman ethnological stock and live in the jungles between Burma and Thailand. They weave fabrics, often in red and black, and embroider them with designs and shells.

THE PROCESS

Most embroidery of the hill-tribe peoples is done on a plain weave cloth where warp and weft threads can be easily counted. The cloth is generally basted in a plain cloth covering to keep it clean, with only the part to be embroidered exposed. The Yao woman works on the back side of the cloth and turns it over when the work has been completed.

Mock Weaving and Cross-stitches

There are three basic stitches used by the Yaos (and Meos). The weave stitch, or running stitch, is a series of parallel lines giving the effect of being woven rather than stitched. It is the oldest of the three stitches and dominates in the execution of the five oldest Yao designs. (These five original designs always appear on the bottom of the women's pants.)

At some point in history, the weave stitch grew into a horizontal cross-stitch where the stitches cross at right angles as in a cross. Each line of the cross-stitch serves the function of continuing into the next, but each unit or cross is stitched separately. Sometimes one or two arms of the cross-stitch are eliminated, as the design requires. The overall effect is a lacy one.

The fabric for embroidery has very definite warp and wefts that are useful in counting cross-stitches. This Yao woman embroiders on the back side of the cloth and turns it over when finished to reveal a full design.

A T'boli woman from Mindanao playing a two-string musical instrument called a "hagalong." Her blouse is embroidered with cross-stitch.

Courtesy: Dottie Anderson

A T'boli woman's blouse designed with cross-stitch.

The third stitch is the diagonal cross-stitch, which looks like an X. Looking on the "wrong" side, both horizontal and diagonal cross-stitches appear to be the same. In the diagonal cross-stitch, each X becomes a dot of color, whereas with the horizontal cross-stitch, the individual stitch is not apparent and seems to become an integral part of the whole. The diagonal cross-stitches are usually executed in three or more colors.

Some stitches are very tightly interrelated and tiny; in others the background cloth (usually black) shows through, better defining the contour and line of the design, with each X being distinctly observable.

A sampler of hill-tribe designs (northern Thailand)—all created with individual cross-stitches that completely fill in the area so that the coarse linen background is not seen.

A close-up of a cross-stitch pattern.

A center pattern of a tablecloth.

A tablecloth runner in cross-stitch.

A repeat pattern in cross-stitch.

Eyeglass cases embroidered in cross-stitch (from northern Thailand).

The hill-tribe people are being encouraged to market their embroidery in many salable forms such as these pillows. It is hoped that their success would eliminate the need to produce opium.

A close-up of a tablecloth centerpiece.

Couching

Couching is the process whereby an independent thread is positioned and then attached to the base fabric by any number of stitches, such as cross-stitches, invisible stitches, etc., using a second thread. This stitch is often called the *Oriental* stitch. Much embroidery is done this way, particularly the remarkable textiles of the Lampong district of South Sumatra.

A close-up showing how gold threads are couched in a checker-board design on a warp-faced, plain weave of blue and brown cotton.

This skirt is from the Lampong district of South Sumatra and is used for ceremonial occasions. Two strips of fabric are sewn together to form a tubelike skirt.

Mrs. Sanuar and family, of Pandai Seikat, Pandang, Sumatra, are restretching a food cover in order to demonstrate the couching embroidery process that she used.

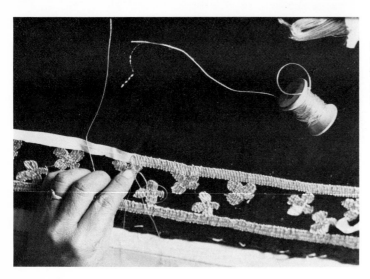

Strips of cut paper serve as pattern and stitch gauge. Gold thread is curved back and forth to fill in the area and then is stitched in place with yellow thread. Eventually the paper is removed.

A completed *tu-tup carano* (food cover) from the Padang Highlands, Sumatra.

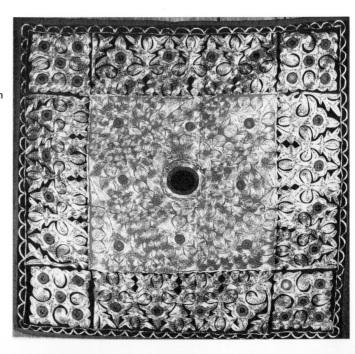

This painting shows a woman of that region of west-central Sumatra in traditional dress standing before containers topped with embroidered food covers.

Satin Stitch and Chinese Filling Stitch

The *satin stitch* is an under-and-over stitch, placed closely, side by side. When short, it is used to outline an area, and when longer, or longer and shorter, as the case may be, it is used to fill in larger areas, most often following a contour and becoming a solidly filled in area with no background fabric visible. When zones of color are used in distinct rows instead of being shaded together, it is called the *Chinese filling* stitch.

A Buginese woman from Sengkang, Sulawesi, embroiders at a frame using silk threads and the satin stitch as in old Chinese embroidery—a tradition that is hundreds of years old.

Appliqué

Appliqué of small pieces of fabric superimposed above a background piece with edges folded under and invisibly stitched is sometimes used in addition to embroidery. In the case of the Meo, batik designs are integrated into the design as well.

Other groups, such as the Balinese and Dayaks, embroider with beads, appliquéing them to a base. Shells are also used by the Karens in conjunction with embroidery. It adds a change of texture and a sense of preciousness to the embroidered design. Sometimes beads or shells are attached one at a time, other times five or ten or more are strung on a thread and then further attached to the background with the same thread or another thread, as in couching.

Small rounds of mica or mirror are appliquéd by using two or more rows of buttonhole (or blanket) stitch, one row looping through the previous one, so that the effect looks almost crocheted. The netlike web encloses the mica, pocketing the piece so it doesn't fall out. In the buttonhole stitch, thread is looped under the point of the needle to form half hitches that are carried along the edge from left to right. The origin for this technique was probably India. The textiles of Lampong (South Sumatra) often employ mica as a part of the embroidered design.

The Meo of northern Thailand create aprons combining batik elements with appliqué and embroidery.

Another repeat design in embroidery and appliqué typical of the Meo.

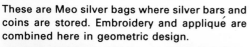

These are Meo silver bags where silver bars and coins are stored. Embroidery and appliqué are combined here in geometric design.

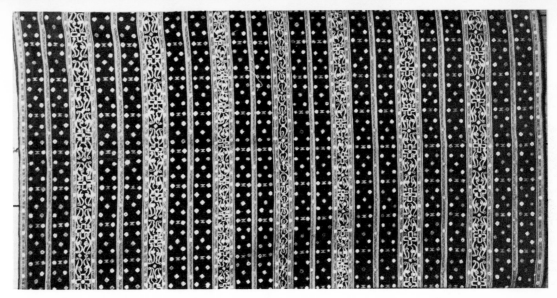

Small rounds of mica are appliquéd on a background using a buttonhole stitch. The other design elements incorporate stripes that are woven into the fabric with co-ordinated embroidery in mock weaving and satin stitches. This skirt is from the Lampong district, Sumatra.

A close-up showing the details of the repeat design.

Some reverse appliqué is employed here, inasmuch as pieces are cut out of an appliquéd shape, revealing a background color. The scrolls and crosses are negative shapes.

3

WEAVING

 OVERVIEW

Almost every form of weaving is found somewhere in Southeast Asia. There is a long tradition of women weaving complex and magnificent fabrics. Much of the weaving is inextricably interwoven with custom. In many societies, such as the Buginese in Sulawesi and the people of Sumba and Bali, a girl is not considered of marriageable age until she can weave proficiently.

Perhaps the most notable of the textiles found in Southeast Asia are ikat weaves, the supplementary warp, inlay such as swivel weaving and other forms of brocade weaving. Remarkable results are achieved with very simple looms, most frequently the backstrap loom.

It is not possible to pinpoint when the ikat technique was introduced to Southeast Asia, but we do know that it emanated from the Dongson and Late Chou cultures. The beautiful silk marriage dresses of Gujarat, which is a double ikat on silk, were traded from Northwest India all the way to Malaysia and Indonesia. These were called the *patola* silks. Both the warp and weft threads are tied and dyed separately in various colors along its length, in precalculated measurements, and arranged on the loom so that as weaving progresses the design takes shape and is the same on both sides of the fabric. In some areas it is called jaspé, chiné, *kasurii* or *kashiri* (in Japan). When both the warp and weft are painted or tie dyed at measured points, it is called *double ikat.* When the warp is tie dyed it is *warp ikat,* and similarly, when the weft is tie dyed, it is called *weft ikat.*

Very little double ikat exists today. One notable example, called geringsing, is found in a mountain village of Tenganan Pegeringsingan in Bali. These textiles are heirlooms in the village and in the rest of Bali. Weft ikat is found today in Thailand, Sumatra, and Sulawesi by the Buginese. And warp ikat is carried out in Sumba, Flores, Roti, Bali, and in Kalimantan by the Dayaks,

A brightly colored contemporary version of the ancient patola silk from Gujarat, India, that inspired so many of the weaving designs of Southeast Asia. Both warp and weft of silk are tied in a rare double ikat process.

Another notable example of double ikat from Tenganan Pegeringsingan in Bali.

in Sulawesi by the Toradjas, and in Mindanao, Philippines by the T'boli people, to name a few places.

The supplementary warp (and sometimes weft) processes of weaving patterns or designs is a means of creating designs without changing the basic or underlying simple weave. In this approach, a second, additional warp (or weft, as the case may be) appears on the surface of the cloth. Usually it is a lighter color than the base warp. The *supplementary warp* "floats" over the background from selvage to selvage. As in ikating, the design usually appears as a lighter color against a dark ground. These processes are a way of creating design in a plain weave where equipment is minimal.

Other ways of introducing pattern into a weave is to pick out a design with fingers or a pick, which results in a laid-in change of color there. Small shuttles of color are carried underneath and color appears on the surface only when desired.

The brocade process would be a supplementary weft with yarn emerging on the surface or face of the fabric as pattern, and when not needed, carried beneath and running from selvage to selvage.

A remarkable cloth headpiece of the Tausug people from Jolo, the Philippines. The warp is striped, forming a grid-type graph, which acts as a guide for the tapestry-like silk weaving.

Warp ikat from Sumba.

Warp ikat using abaca from Mindanao, the Philippines.
Courtesy: Dottie Anderson

A man's belt from Malaysia in
a supplementary warp pattern.

Two special silk weft on a cotton warp weavings from Thailand. The effect looks as if
it is embroidered when in fact it is a laid-in process, in which many small shuttles of silk
color are used with the silk appearing on the cotton surface when desired.

Ulas (cloth) of the Batak people of Lumba Garaga, North Sumatra, woven in a brocade process. It is a warp pattern with the warp set closely. The filling is brown and travels from selvage to selvage. We see the filling where the pattern is picked up. A few spots of rust color are inlaid in certain areas.

Details of the ulas. The weft is carried beneath when not appearing on the face of the cloth and runs from selvage to selvage.   The fringe is plied fringe; twisted very tightly and tied at the bottom.

THE BASIC WEAVING PROCESS

Before the discovery of the downy substance called cotton and the unraveled cocoon called silk, bark cloth and bast fibers (consisting of grasses and leaves), and later sheep and other animal skins, were the principal textile materials. As soon as it was discovered that fibers could be twisted into threads and that they could be woven much like grasses, did the textile making art of weaving emerge. Certainly weaving is one of the oldest crafts known to mankind. People needed something to cover their naked skin. It was a component of mankind's need for shelter. As soon as people were able to protect themselves from their environment and some fear for survival was mitigated by this protection, embellishment and decoration of home and body followed. People wanted to be as decorative as nature; as colorful and richly textured as birds, animals, and plants.

Authorities claim that plaiting and basketry preceded weaving and were the precursors to the simple harness loom. The most elementary fabric consists of numerous threads running parallel, called a *warp,* and threads woven in and out at right angles to the warp, called the *weft.* This forms a continuous *web* or cloth. It is possible to manipulate these threads with fingers alone, but virtually every society has devised some form of loom—a frame or strips of wood to facilitate the interweaving of fibers.

In order to interweave the weft threads, devices called shuttles were used. Some way also was developed to raise alternate numbers of warp threads so that the shuttle could be passed through, back and forth, looping around each of the end warp threads to create a selvage and thereby hold the web (fabric from the loom) together.

This "belt" loom of the Buginese from Sulawesi probably preceded the backstrap loom. Each end is tied to a tree or post. The heddles operate as levers of a scale, tipping up and down.

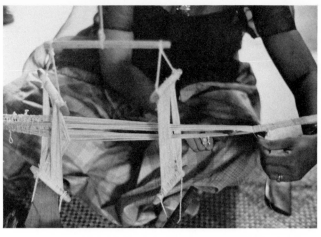

Warp is strung through . . .

. . . and then beaten closely together with a paddle-like sword or batten.

It was discovered that by riding weft threads over two or three warp threads (or whatever) in a metrical arrangement, patterns could be created. Means were developed to raise specific groups of warp threads. In various areas of Southeast Asia, through use of a shed stick to which the warp was attached or by means of cord heddles (string loops), people learned to raise and lower specific warp threads. Then gold and silver threads and other color threads could be passed through to create a pattern. It was also possible to introduce an extra warp (or weft) of different colors that appeared only when picked up by special shed sticks.

Some examples of belts made on this ancient loom.

Bontoc Igorot backstrap weavings contain symbols. Note the tattoo on the weaver s arms. Here she is picking out the pattern.

The pattern is lifted by raising the pattern stick.

Here the shed is being cleared. (The beads on her head are thought to impart good luck.)

A shuttle is run through. Three different warps, each with different colors, are being woven at the same time.

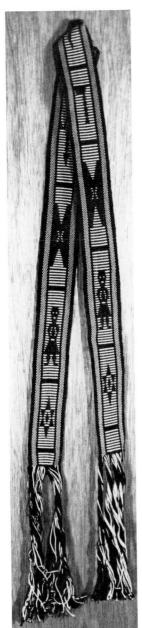

An Igorot belt from Luzon, the Philippines. Patterns have symbolic meanings. The star means ethereal protection; the man symbolizes life; the shield and arrow indicate physical protection.

A close-up detailing star, man, arrow, and shield.

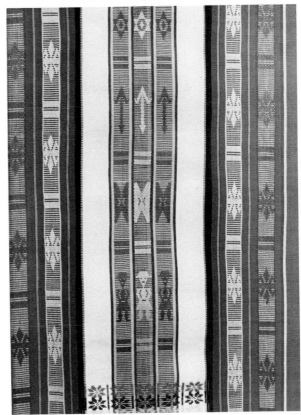

The Backstrap Loom

One of the most common and the simplest horizontal loom is the *backstrap loom.* Warp yarns are held taut between a tree, post, or some fixed object and the body of the weaver. A strap, attached to a stick at the front of the loom, passes around the weaver's back at the waist or below, hence the term "backstrap." By shifting her weight, the weaver can control the tension of the yarn.

Note the parts of a typical backstrap loom in the diagram shown here.

ONE TYPE OF BACKSTRAP LOOM.

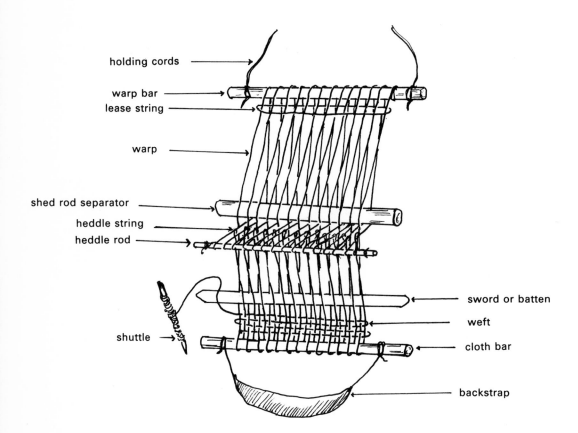

There are many variations of backstrap looms from Norway to Africa, to Ecuador, to Hawaii, and Southeast Asia. Versions of these looms are found virtually everywhere in the world. Variations are found in how the shedding system is created—that space determined by the lifting and lowering of warp threads so that the shuttle can be drawn through. A sword or beater is used to beat each row of yarn against the previously woven part.

The backstrap loom can be as wide or as narrow as one can manage. The width determines how wide the fabric will be. It can be as narrow as a belt or 40 inches wide. A comfortable width is 22 to 24 inches. The length of fabric is determined by how long the warp threads are in the first place, making allowance for a fringe, or waste at each end when there isn't enough space for the shuttle. As weaving progresses, the woven cloth is wrapped or rolled around the front stick or rod, called the *cloth stick,* which is next to the body.

If you would like to construct a very simple version of a backstrap loom, it can be accomplished by gluing together a slot and eye heddle (as illustrated here), using tongue depressors. Note that holes are drilled in the centers of each tongue depressor to accommodate one group of warp threads, and spaces are left for the alternate warp threads. By lifting the heddle, a shed is formed with only one group of threads being lifted at a time. Through this shed, the shuttle, which is a small stick or piece of cardboard wrapped with yarn, is passed through from right to left; the heddle is then lowered, creating a new shed, and the shuttle is returned in the opposite direction, from the left to the right. An even tension should be allowed so that the selvage (outside edges) are straight and not uneven. This operation continues until the cloth, or web, builds.

Preparation for Weaving

After the loom has been readied, the warp yarns need to be measured so that they are all the same length. This can be done by winding the warp around two chairs, set at the distance you desire, perhaps two or three yards. The number of turns around the chair is determined by how many slots and holes are in the heddle. To simplify the later threading of the loom, two sticks should be stuck into the ground, or mounted in such a way as to allow for a cross to be made (see illustration). Before cutting the warp, a cord or a 1/2-inch dowel should be slipped through one part of the cross and cord should be attached to each end, keeping the warp from sliding off. The other rod is strung through the other space and tied with cord the same way. These are called *lease sticks.* Cord can be used instead to create this temporary separation.

Holding the warp firmly, separate them by cutting the warp between both fingers and form a temporary slipknot of the warp at one end, the part to be tied later to the cloth sticks—a 1-inch dowel to which your backstrap is attached. Then string the loose ends of the warp through the heddle slots and holes (eyes), using the alternate sequence prescribed by the cross that is held temporarily by the lease sticks.

If you have used lease sticks, slide these toward the slip-knotted end and release the slipknot. Then in small groups of two or three, slip-knot the ends around a 1-inch dowel, the cloth stick. The lease sticks can remain in place to maintain a spread of the warp.

Around each end of the dowel (a notch helps), tie a belt or strap that can be held comfortably around your body and not so close that your arms are cramped. Tie the other end of the warp to a doorknob, bedpost, or something rigid that is higher up than you at a sitting position.

Now, by lifting and lowering the heddle, your shed is created, and by leaning backward or forward you can control tension. Weaving begins. If you pass the shuttle through the warp near to the heddle, no stick or sword needs to be used to maintain the opening. But a sword or beater should be used to beat each weft line to the body of the weaving. A large coarse-toothed haircomb can be used, or a long smooth stick with ends sanded into a smooth, rounded blade.

A very simple backstrap loom for weaving narrow widths. From Lake Lanao area, Marawi, Mindanao, the Philippines. Used by the Maranao people to weave decorative strips for the malong (tubular dress).

Weft is threaded through with fingers, in and out of the warp, in order to achieve a particular pattern.

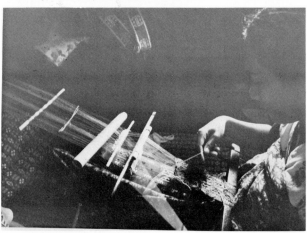

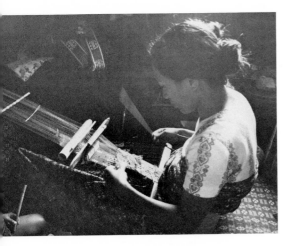

Ends of individual weft colors are left exposed and hanging. The part you are looking at is the wrong side.

A malong, which is a tubular dress. The decorative strips, woven on the single backstrap loom shown here, were sewn among three wider widths of fabric.

A very crude heddle, made of tongue depressors, for a backstrap loom. Note that the cardboard strips, in the foreground, help separate warp. The wooden strip is used to tie string to it and around the waist of the weaver.

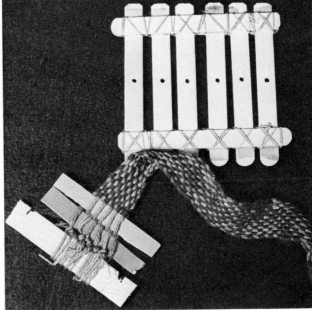

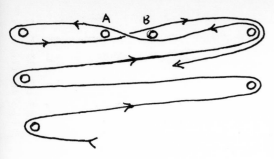

To simplify threading of the loom later, warp is strung around sticks as indicated by the direction arrows. Threads cross at *A* and *B*, determining alternate warp threads. Later, lease sticks or a lease cord is strung through *A* and around through *B*. The length of the warp is determined by how many times the warp is strung before crossing at *A* and *B*.

After practicing weaving, more control is attained. Try picking designs and adding a supplementary warp or weft or laid-in weft. Amazingly intricate patterns can be created with this simple loom. It does not seem possible that almost all the textiles shown here were done on a backstrap loom!

Now that you have had a weaving experience, you may wish to construct an authentic loom, much like the ones used in Southeast Asia. "Redwood" wrote and illustrated an excellent how-to booklet giving exact details for constructing a traditional backstrap loom, how to thread the loom, and weave with it. An inexperienced person will succeed by following the specific instructions in "The Loom Book," 318 Pacheco Street, Santa Cruz, California 95060 ($4.25).

Of course, very complicated, multiharness floor looms are used in parts of Southeast Asia. This is still handweaving, but on a more sophisticated level, and usually it is carried out in small shops or cooperatives.

DESCRIPTION OF SPECIFIC TEXTILES

Warp Ikats of the Lesser Sunda Islands, Indonesia

THE LORE

Threads, looms, and the results of weaving often have religious significance. To the people of the Lesser Sunda Islands, the act of weaving has many rituals. As a result, fabrics are important documents of the area's culture. The weaver, always a woman, has to pick an auspicious time to work, and while she is working she may not talk to men and men may not be present. She often prays, burns incense, or makes offerings to the loom and the spirits.

Textiles of each of the Lesser Sunda Islands have their own styles and motifs and colors. Though some designs are purely ornamental, such as those from Sawu, and Flores, others bear complex relationships to the society. In Sumba there is a feeling for dramatic visual effect and motifs have specific and powerful significance. The crocodile on a hinggi (cloth for clothing or ceremonies) may serve at funeral rites as a symbol for passage to another world. In Sawu, there is a commonly occurring rose meander that is arranged between more simply decorated stripes, and contrary to the horizontal arrangement of bands of design in Sumbaese hinggi, these are divided vertically. Hinggi in Sumba are always woven of cotton in pairs and their symbols can be read starting from the bottom fringe up. Tones are strong in blue, red, brown, and tan; ikating is precise; the weave is tight and Z-shaped stitches join the two panels. These are used as men's ceremonial clothing, are used in their elaborate funeral ceremonies, and serve as elements in ritual gift exchange systems.

Sumbaese ruling families save many of their finest hinggi for dressing the corpse and draping them until they form a huge mound. Relatives and friends bring textiles as funeral gifts. These are displayed at the funeral by the hundreds. It is a demonstration of power and wealth, and their perpetuation by the family.

Techniques of dyeing, which produced deep intensities of the traditional colors, were jealously guarded in Sumba. This was the province of the nobility. Once only the wealthy nobility had the time and could afford the slaves to help with the weaving after the noblewoman had completed the secret dyeing process. Only the very rich could afford to replace cloths lost to ritual exchanges for visits, marriages, and the funerals spoken about earlier.

Today, though some women dye and weave for income, most do their weaving between other family chores. Precise skill and much patience are required for ikating. It may take several months to make a Sumba hinggi, and up to eight years for a Balinese geringsing. Although ready-made threads and chemical dyes are more available, the woman may substitute purchased thread rather than spin her own, but use of chemical dyes is frowned upon as being inferior. After all the work and skill that go into ikating, it is thought a pity that chemical dyes are used when the natural dyes grow right in the area.

THE PROCESS

Ikating is essentially the same wherever it is done. Some of the basic implements might vary somewhat; dyeing and dyes and their colors are different—but the concept is the same. Ikating is a resist process. Areas of yarn are tied off to resist the penetration of dye in precisely the spot where figures are to appear when the loom is threaded (for warp ikating) or where the weft passes through the warp. Both take a great deal of planning, measuring, practice, and skill.

Preparation of Cotton

Cotton fiber is the most usual material for ikating, followed by silk. Cotton yarn is spun either with a spindle or with a simple spinning wheel. After spinning, the threads are "filled" by immersing them in the baths of grated cassava (a starchy, potato-like food staple), rice gruel, or meal made from roasted corn. Then the thread is wound onto a winder. In some cases, the smoothness and fineness approximate machine-spun varieties.

Tieing and Dyeing

After the white yarn is prepared, the yarn has to be warped. This is done by winding the warp yarn around a binding frame for the purpose of tieing off parts of the warp into a design. The frame is usually a rectangle or square formed by two long bamboo poles or tubes with crossbars inset at both ends and two cords tied (that act as built-in flexible lease sticks) near one end to create the alternate warp for a shed. The yarn is placed in a coconut shell or bowl and is drawn from there, passed by two women sitting within the frame. From hand to hand, they run the yarn across the frame and alternately over and under two cords tied across the frame, and over the end crossbars. There is then an upper and lower layer of continuous circular warp, divided into odd

Warp yarn is tied around a binding frame. Sets of warp threads are then tightly tied off with polyethylene or raffia string.

Ends of each string used for wrapping are tightly tied or knotted.

Another warp in process. Note the lease string above the roosters.

Tied cotton warp that has been dyed is left to dry before unbinding areas and stringing the loom.

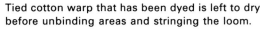

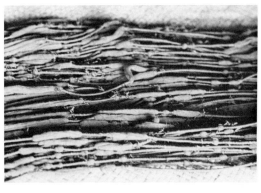

and even strands for later threading of the loom. Six to ten of these strands are usually grouped together into a set and are kept separate by twisting the cross cords between each set. These become the basic units for the resist tieing. A second panel is superimposed on the frame and its upper layer is bundled together to match the first panel. Each panel consists of two parts that are later sewn together and two complete identical units are made requiring four parts.

For tieing, strips of palm leaf, or raffia, once was used, but today polyethylene wrapping twine, that very well duplicates the flatness and resistance of raffia to water, is used to tightly tie off patterns. The background usually is dyed first and the design appears as a positive shape. Sometimes designs are in the negative or in a darker color, requiring the entire background to be tied instead of the outlines and body of the designs. This takes more time and is more rare.

Women do not use pattern guides; they have learned their skills well and execute patterns from memory. Usually, the Sumba hinggi are dyed in two colors, creating variations in color as they overlap or mix and by the length of time threads are left to steep in the dye. On some islands, when two colors are used, the warp does not have to be tied more than one time because different knots are used in the tieing to distinguish the parts of the pattern to be colored differently. After each dyeing stage, the proper knots are released, revealing another open area for receiving the new color. But in Sumba, each color requires dyeing and then replacing of the warp on the frame for tieing of new areas.

The result of the sequence is that some areas appear to be medium blue, others are white, some are rust (kombu) and some are a purple-like brown, the result of mixing together the indigo (blue) and kombu (rust). The warp is then dipped or bathed with stiffener (the cassava starch mixture) and is hung on a frame for stretching, still containing the crossbands of cotton cord to keep the warp divided into odd and even strands for threading the loom.

Blue dye derives from indigo plants, which are quite plentiful. The twigs from the indigo plant (wora) are cooked in a pot with water. The solution is allowed to stand for a day and then it is strained through a plaited sieve made of lontar leaf. The water is drained off and the twigs are saved. These are dried and kept. To use the wora (indigo twigs), a solution of water and ashes (lye is in ashes and acts as a mordant) is mixed together. The ashes are allowed then to sink and the water is poured into a pot containing the wora. The tied warp is then dipped into this dye over and over again until the proper intensity of color is obtained.

For the rust color, the bark and roots of the kombu tree (*Morinda citrifolia*) are used. To achieve this color, the warp has to be soaked in a bark solution containing tannin (the same as for treating hides). Then the oil from plants is stamped into the warp several times, with alternate intervals of drying in the sun. The dyestuff (kombu) comes from drying and pounding the smaller roots and only the rind from larger roots. The pounded roots are further softened in water and the sediment is discarded. The fabric is soaked in water containing dyestuff and alum, the mordant, and the dyeing process is complete. Credits to all this dedication! How simple it would be to use aniline dyes.

Kombu plant, shown behind the girl, produces a rust-colored dye.

Indigo, shown here, provides the other basic color of the Sumba weavings.

The Weaving Process for Ikat

The essential elements of the backstrap loom used to weave ikat hinggi consist of two lightweight bamboo tubes. One, the warp beam, is attached by cords to two posts and is held horizontally slightly above the ground; the other is parallel to it and serves as the cloth beam which rests in front of the weaver. This beam is attached on each end by cords to a piece of wood carved to fit the contours of the weaver's back. This is the backstrap.

Weaving is usually done outside in the shade or under the house. The loom is set up or strung by attaching the warp beam and the cloth beams to a frame. The warp yarn is then passed from around one beam to another in a continuous fashion, with the distance between the beams measuring half the length of the cloth to be woven. Broken threads are now repaired by tieing. It is a continuous warp, uncut at this point. Earlier, odd and even yarns had been separated; with this accomplished, the separation is further ensured by the insertion of lease rods. Then small loops of cord are attached to a heddle rod and through these loops the odd warp yarn is threaded, with the even yarn strung between the loops. A sword or beater is used to compress the weft as it is woven, making the weave firm and tight, and is used to enlarge the shed. Because the yarn tension is controlled by the backward pressure of the weaver's body, there is a limit to the length of the warp—which is usually about three meters long (almost 3 ½ yards), and the width is about 50 to 65 centimeters (almost 20 to 26 inches). The warp pattern dominates, with the weft receding in a plain weave. To do this, the weft threads are not tightly compressed.

Weaving a hinggi in process, under a house, in the shade. The warp is continuous. Four lengths, each woven separately, produce a pair.

The ikat cloth from other islands, such as Sawu, are also warp-faced weaves using similar vegetable dyes. The dark grounds are distinguished by small designs where there is slight bleeding around edges caused by dye seeping under the edges of the bindings.

An ikat weaving from Sumba. Two lengths are sewn together. Two of these are sold together.

Another warp ikat weaving from Sumba.

A Sumba hinggi with stripes.

A shawl woven in warp ikat from Sawu, Indonesia.

Warp ikat from Flores, Indonesia.

Weft Ikat by the Buginese of Sengkang, Sulawesi, the Balinese of Granjar, Bali, and the Thais

In weft ikat, the continuous weft thread is tied in a similar manner as in reserving the yarn for warp ikat. The weft is wound on a frame that approximates the width of the cloth to be woven. The pattern is tied in small bundles, removed from the frame, and dyed, or, as in Bali, painted with naphthol, the mordant, and then brushed with dye in the appropriate areas. Since patterns have to match when woven through the warp, they are wound from a wheel to the shuttle. A rotation of the wheel approximates the width of the cloth and each pass of the shuttle. If all starting points correspond, the shadowy pattern of the weft ikat emerges. With some minor adjustments made by pulling the weft slightly in one direction or another at the selvage, the design corresponds easily.

The Buginese women of Sengkang, Sulawesi (Celebes), tell a story of silk's arrival and the idea for their sarong weaving. The gods, they said, were bathing in magnificent Lake Tempe and left their divine sarongs on the shore. People discovered the fabrics, imitated the heavenly cloth, and have been weaving the fine silk sarongs ever since.

Historians tell another version of the Buginese myth. Indian migrations spread the use of the sarong, a tube of cloth four feet wide and six feet long, through all of Southeast Asia. Travels of the Chinese, Thais, and Cambodians brought the fine, uncolored silk thread to Sulawesi during the same period. (There is also a strong similarity to weft silk weaving of Thailand and the Thai sarong.)

Weavers themselves prepare the silk fibers now, growing, harvesting, and unwinding the cocoons. Girl children assist in learning the art. Barks, reeds, leaves, roots, and spices lend their dyes to color the threads.

Not too many decades ago special designs belonged to the nobility, other patterns were donned at festivals, and still others could be worn by anyone, every day. Only women weave here, too. And weaving became one of the marriageable skills. Proficiency as a weaver signified maturity. Weaving cloth was an important part of a woman's dowry, her tangible wealth. It became a sign of social grace and station.

Though Sengkanese silks remain a traditional art form, it never has been a static one. Designs change with new influences. New dyes are imported; new looms are being introduced. Yet the Sengkanese silk is being woven now as much as before. It takes a full week to weave a sarong.

Cocoons of the silkworm and raw unspun silk.   Silkworms grown on branches are ready for "harvesting."

Unspun silk being twisted into fine threads.

Silk in hanks, ready for stringing on a loom or for dyeing.

Silk being dyed by a Buginese woman from Sengkang, Sulawesi.

Warp tied for dyeing in an ikat pattern.

The warp is being strung.

Here the ikated weft is rotated so that, as it is wound on the shuttle, each pass of the weft pattern will coordinate with previous and future rows of thread.

A warp beam is being wrapped with warp thread prior to being attached to the loom. This beam slides into slots at the foot of the loom as shown . . .

... here. This loom is another version of the backstrap loom. Note that the body is required to apply pressure to keep the warp taut. This loom was probably a precursor of the floor loom.

The ikat weft is adjusted at the selvage to ensure proper alignment of the pattern.

The warp of the Sengkanese ikat silk sarong is usually solid or striped. Designs and patterns appear in pastel, bright and dark colors—a full range. With a few exceptions, only one part of the sarong, the section that appears in the front, is in ikat. A sarong consists of two parallel lengths, sewn together to form the full skirt length.

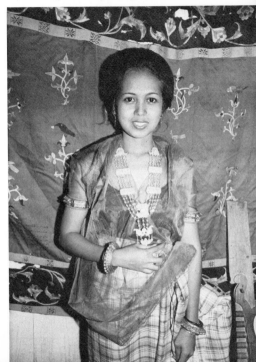

A Buginese woman from Sengkang, Sulawesi, in traditional dress. The silk embroidery on the wall is Chinese.

An example of a length for a sarong of Sengkanese silk. The fabric is cut in half and sewn together with zigzag patterns matching. This differently patterned area is folded as a front pleat of the sarong.

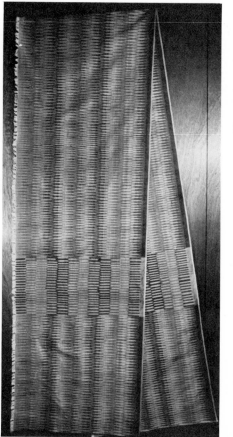

Another traditional pattern in blues and violets. Sengkanese sarongs are an essential part of a young woman's dowry. Not only is it a measure of her wealth; it is also a sign of social grace and station. Note that unlike the plaids shown here, this entire sarong is ikat dyed.

A detail.

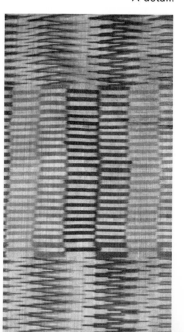

Weft ikat marriage cloth of the Bataks, North Sumatra.

In Bali, the ikat material (*kamben endek*) more often is a shadow of the old tradition, with design greatly simplified and colors reduced in intensity. Lower in the hierarchy of textiles and worn for everyday wear, there was a relaxation of rules for the weaving of these cloths.

The silk weft ikat of Thailand did not go through such a metamorphosis of a design as in Bali; rather, the process was speeded up with use of commercial dyes (as in Bali) and the use of more complex looms (also as in Bali). The flying shuttle is also in operation. Nevertheless, weaving is still very much a handcraft and weaving these beautiful fabrics still is a painfully slow process. Very little is exported. The price is so high that only very rich Thai women can afford sarongs of silk ikat.

Tieing *kamben endek,* weft ikat of Bali.

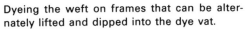

Dyeing the weft on frames that can be alternately lifted and dipped into the dye vat.

Dipping the weft into a mordant to fix the color.

Rinsing the weft after dyeing.

Allowing the dyed weft to dry in the sun.

Untieing the ikated weft.

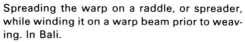

Spreading the warp on a raddle, or spreader, while winding it on a warp beam prior to weaving. In Bali.

Measuring out lengths of ikated weft.

Releasing some weft from the shuttle before . . .

. . . passing it through on a fly shuttle loom. This is a plain weave.

A Balinese woman wearing the weft ikat sarong. Note the rainbow tie-and-dye belt.

Tieing the silk weft in an ikat pattern typical of Thailand.

A bundled, tied silk weft waiting to be dyed.

The weft ikat being woven, in Thailand, on a wide floor loom.

Note that there is no flying shuttle and that the weaver has to "coax" the shuttle through.

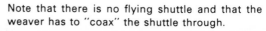
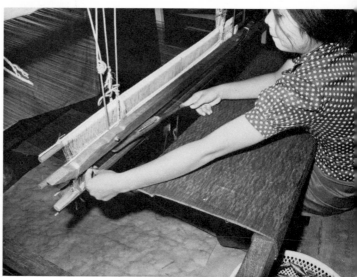

Detail of a finely woven silk weft ikat fabric from Thailand. Colors are black, gold, and rust.

Another weft ikat pattern. Thailand.

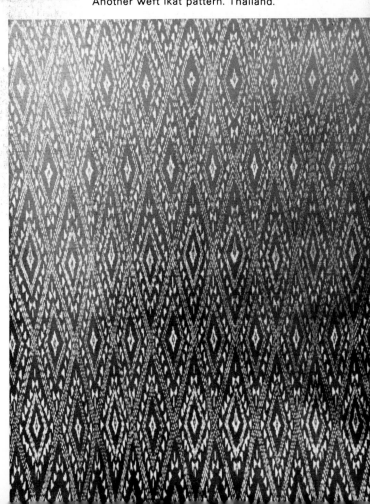

Weft and Warp Ikat—the Geringsing of Tenganan, Pegeringsingan, Bali

Weft and warp ikat is the most difficult and the most rare kind of ikat weaving, particularly the intricate *geringsing,* as this is called in Bali. These are the most highly respected textiles in the hierarchy of skill and made only within the walls of a mountain village called Tenganan Pegeringsingan. Every insect-eaten scrap is revered and saved as a treasure. They are so valued that they are patched and used for all kinds of ceremonies—cutting of the first lock of hair, for tooth-filing, treatment of the sick, for covering the dead at the wake in the house. The unwoven part of the continuous warp of a completed geringsing is cut as part of the marriage ceremony. Geringsing means "illness averting" in Balinese. It is definitely a powerful fabric. Each occasion demands cloths of different patterns.

The remarkable warp and weft ikat of Tenganan called *geringsing.* Here the warp has been tied with strips of dried grass.

Once dyed, bundles of warp and weft are left to hang for years until the colors have oxidized to their desired hue.

One bundle has been untied and is ready for weaving.

The geringsing is woven on a backstrap loom in a plain weave. Here the sword is being inserted between warp threads to help open the shed.

The shuttle containing the weft threads is placed in a bamboo tube and ...

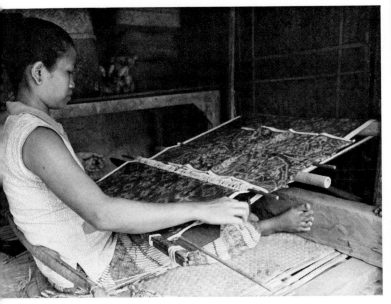

... is passed through to the other side of the fabric.

The sword is used to beat weft threads tightly together.

Any inconsistencies in pattern-matching are adjusted.

Here the Tenganese weaver is pulling up the warp so it can be moved forward while the string heddles are moved back somewhat.

The weaver is admiring another pattern that she has woven.

Perhaps one reason the geringsing is so revered is that it is so difficult to make and so time consuming. It may take eight years from start to finish of a geringsing because of the rituals surrounding both the dyeing and weaving processes. It was said that human blood was once used in the dyes. Although no longer true, the cloths do still look as if they are the color of dried blood —a dark maroon brown. In order to achieve this effect, once the ikated warp and weft have been dyed, they are left to hang for years until the color has oxidized and turned to the desired hue. This also greatly weakens the fibers. They break easily, making the weaving process all the more laborious because the warp-and-weft fibers have to be tied precisely. Nevertheless, if any aspect of this process is to change, then the cloth will have less power and, commensurately, less importance in religious ceremonies.

The process of ikat dyeing and weaving, as we can see in the photographs, is essentially the same as it is in Sumba. So is the material, cotton. Even the backstrap loom is similar. The essential difference lies in the style of motif and in color. Sometimes, more rarely now, the ends of the geringsing, which is worn over the breast, were woven with gold threads in a brocade weave.

Two traditional geringsing fabrics that people believe contain potent powers.

Warp Ikat of the T'boli, Mindanao, Philippines

THE LORE

The T'boli people of Mindanao, Philippines, weave the T'nalak, which is a fibrous fabric woven in the same way for centuries. It is used basically for blankets and clothing, but has deeper significance for T'boli people. It is used as part of an exchange at marriage, and when a woman gives birth, it is considered conducive to safe delivery to use the T'nalak as a covering. It is also used at certain feasts. The T'boli feel that if you cut the cloth you will become seriously ill or die. Often they attach a brass ring to the cloth before selling it, to appease the spirits.

Patterns have many symbols—leaves of trees, shields, frogs, snakes, man in his house, a fast-flying large bird from the sea, and so on.

THE PROCESS

Fibers come from a fruit-bearing abaca plant that is about 18 months old and at least 10 feet tall. The fibers are stripped by hand from the soft, moist pulp of the abaca stalk. Through repeated combing and bleaching in the sun, the fibers become pliable and flaxen.

To tie-dye the fibers in the ikat process, the warp is laid out on a simple loom. One end is woven a few inches to fix the fibers during the dyeing process. (Later this portion is cut off and discarded.) With the fibers stretched out, they are then tied in patterns with other abaca fibers that have been coated with beeswax. All areas not to be dyed are tied.

No measuring is employed except with finger joints and parts of the hand and arm. Patterns emerge from women's heads with utmost precision.

After the abaca warp has been tied, the fibers are dyed. The black dye is made from leaves and the red brown from roots of trees.

Fibers are placed in a "double-boiler," which is actually one earthenware pot placed on top of the other. The bundle of tied threads is placed in the upper pot where the steam carries the dye to the fiber. The pot boils hour after hour, for as long as three weeks for black (or very dark brown) and two days for red. The steam is never hot enough to melt the wax used to tie the warp.

The black is dyed first, and then some waxed strings are removed and the newly exposed parts are dyed the reddish brown. With dyeing completed, the remaining strings are untied, revealing the natural cream color of the fiber. The fibers are then rinsed and when dry, laid out again on the loom.

The weft thread has already been dyed the black or dark brown and wrapped on a shuttle.

Weaving is done in a standard plain weave (with warp threads dominating) on a backstrap loom. The backstrap is made of woven rattan and is essentially the same as most backstrap looms of this area.

Most often, weaving is performed at night when the cool air helps keep the fibers most pliable. Often small bells are hung on the edges of the unfinished cloth to frighten away evil spirits while the weaver is weaving.

A T'boli woman ties a warp of abaca.

The tied abaca is awaiting the dye pot.

The dyed warp, after steeping in dye for days, is being removed from the dye pot. *Photos Courtesy: Dottie Anderson*

The warp ikat abaca is being woven.

Note the unique notched bar in the foreground that functions as a "reed" to keep warp fibers evenly spaced.

After being sewn together, the woven fabric, called T'nalak, is pounded with a wooden mallet to soften it.
Photos Courtesy: Dottie Anderson

After the cloth is woven, it is removed from the loom and sewn together, if it is to be a blanket, edge to edge with invisible stitches. The cloth is then pounded with a mallet and rubbed with a cowrie seashell to impart a waxen sheen. The completed cloth takes about two and one-half months to make and is about eighteen feet long.

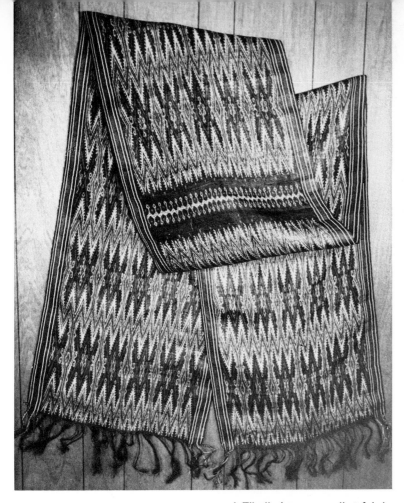

A T'boli abaca warp ikat fabric.

A close-up showing the fine, precise overall design.

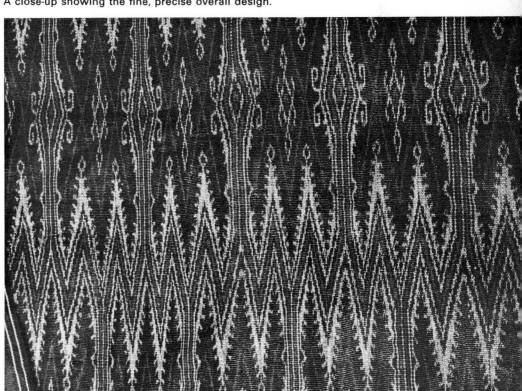

A detail of another T'boli abaca cloth.

A T'boli man wearing the T'nalak cloth.
Photo Courtesy: Dottie Anderson

Yakan of Basilan and Mindanao, Philippine Weaving

The Yakans are a group of people who live on an island southwest of Mindanao called Basilan. They still dress (for ceremonies) in brightly colored fabrics that they weave themselves on a variety of backstrap looms in a range of techniques. The women, here too, are the weavers. The materials they use range from abaca and pineapple fibers to cotton and, more rarely, silk.

Yakans, traditionally of Basilan, the Philippines (now living in Mindanao), weave a variety of fine fabrics. Here a Yakan woman strings her warp. She measures the length of it and counts the number of threads in the width.

The thin stick near her right hand will have the heddle cords attached to it later.

The cross for the warp is made around these "lease" sticks.

The shed is open for the plain-weave background of this tightly woven cotton Yakan weaving.

The shuttle is going to be passed through the open shed. In this fabric the warp pattern dominates because it is set very closely. The weft is a solid color filler.

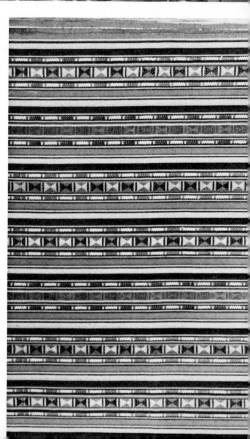

A helper lifts the string heddles to position the proper aspect of pattern. Note the thin bamboo pattern sticks. The pattern sticks are removed after each weaving and are reinserted if the pattern is to be repeated, as is the case here.

The completed Yakan fabric with a pattern that is seven threads high and a mirror or reverse image of it repeated.

The Yakan backstrap loom is about the widest I have seen. It takes a great deal of strength to weave on this loom.

Some weaving, such as the tightly woven striped mercerized cotton cloth used by men for their trousers, has a warp predominating pattern. The warp is very closely set with the pattern picked out using bamboo sticks, slivers or nerves, or palm leaf spines that look like long skewers. This permits the use of one heddle bar, which is a rod tied to the warp with cords looped around alternate warp threads. The bar, alternately lifted and released, provides the plain weave while the sticks, when lifted, pull up a specific pattern. The weft is a fine thread that disappears in the dominant warp. After a particular stick has been used, it is removed and rethreaded into a specific pattern behind the other sticks to make for a continuous pattern. This may be done after many sticks have been removed.

Other weaving of the Yakan is inlay, laid-in, or supplementary weft weaving. Small pattern units are woven at intervals in the warp, usually in different colors for each pattern. Some term this as true brocade. It is called *dukagang* in Scandinavia. Small shuttles are used to carry the pattern threads back and forth within a specific area. When many patterns are used in different colors, there are many shuttles each bearing different colors. The number of colors used is unlimited. The designs usually are geometric and permit zigzag effects.

For this type of weaving, an additional string heddle rod is necessary to lift alternate groups of warp for the laid-in (inlay) pattern section, and the usual one for the filled-in or plain weave. It is placed in front of the one or two regular heddle devices. The string loops on the special heddle for laid-in patterns must be longer to allow the plain (tabby) sheds to form through them.

Another type of weaving performed by the Yakan (and by the Thais), and very rarely, is one that is almost indistinguishable from embroidery. This weave actually stands halfway between weaving and embroidery. It cannot be classified as true embroidery because, in embroidery, thread is applied to previously woven cloth. In this case, the embroidery is integrated into the weaving process. Sometimes a needle is used to carry the extra weft colors.

Specific warp threads are lifted by pulling up string heddles in certain patterns.

An example of a Yakan laid-in (or inlay) weaving.

The weft colors are inserted for each color, while the background filler is woven from selvage to selvage.

No additional brocade heddles are needed with this process. Weft yarn is wrapped around one to four warp threads. The threads may be carried under four warp threads and returning over two—then under four and reversing again over two, or in some other pattern. This continues throughout the row. And a row of plain weave is run through the shed between each row of "embroidered" weaving. Very often ends of the different colored threads are left hanging underneath or on the back of the cloth. Sometimes the ends are knotted.

Called *seputangan,* this is a finely woven silk fabric, used as a belt by the Yakans.

At the funeral bier of the Yakans, precious weavings are laid across the body.
Photo Courtesy: Dottie Anderson

Brocade Weaving Variations—Campo Islam, Mindanao, Philippines

In the village of Campo Islam there are only one or two old people left who know how to do brocade weaving, and there is no one interested anymore in learning this skill. This backstrap loom weaving process is similar to that practiced by the Yakans, except that their bamboo sticks (nerves) are not used to pick up the pattern. Instead, threads tied to specific warp yarn hang loosely, sitting on top of the warp. These are picked up as needed and a shed stick is inserted so that weft can be passed through. The pattern is tightly beaten so that warp threads are not visible except in areas where a warp pattern is desired. This brocade is usually in two colors—warp and weft, with the weft traveling from selvage to selvage.

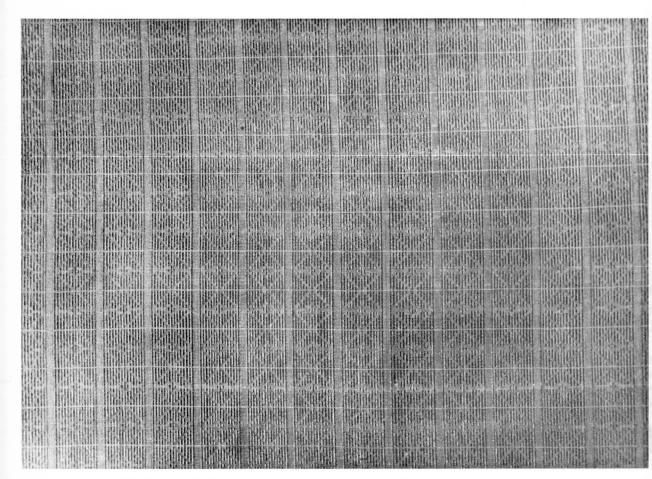

It is difficult to see the fine gradations of pattern on this silk fabric made by supplementary floating warp weaving.

Sumbaese Supplementary Warp Weaving

In Sumba, geometric figures are woven in a twill weave (passing over two successive weft threads) using a supplementary warp. This second additional or supplementary warp appears on the surface of the cloth only where needed to form the design. When not appearing on the face of the cloth, the supplementary warp floats on the reverse side. A tabby or plain weave fills in the rest of the background.

Another supplementary warp process. Here the Marapu weave is from Prailiu, near Waingapu, Sumba, Indonesia. Old patterns, such as the one seen here, are passed down from generation to generation. The weaver has indicated on the pattern with a bamboo sliver where she had left off the last time she was weaving.

The weaver is getting ready to insert a second shed stick that . . .

. . . opens up the supplementary warp pattern.

The pattern shed plain-weave heddles are lifted at the same time and the weft is run through.

A second background shed is lifted, as the process repeats.

The sword is used to beat each row to the area of the fabric already woven.

Pattern sticks are being moved back on the warp to make more room in front of the heddle.

The Sumba supplementary warp process weaving completed. Note that the warp is the pattern and is picked up in addition to the regular warp when the weaver wants the pattern to appear on the face of the cloth; otherwise, it floats on the back of the cloth.

The backstrap loom is set up with two circular warps, the basic warp of a thinner and darker color (which forms the background) and the supplementary warp (which becomes the pattern) of a thicker, lighter color yarn. The pattern yarn is then attached to a second heddle and separated from the basic yarn by a bamboo stick or roller. A large number of thin bamboo sticks (nerves) are laced into the warp creating the pattern. These sticks are then used in succession, one after the other, in combination with the two string-tied heddle rods that in turn form the shed (opening) of the "twill" weave for the weft passes. These sticks also serve to guide the weaver in separating the warps according to the needs of the weaving pattern. After this pattern unit has been woven, the sticks, which have been removed, are threaded into the warp again, following a separate independent design or model of the pattern (that had been designed by a noblewoman), and the pattern is repeated. (Note the pattern in the photos.) To maintain even tension of the basic warp, bundles of sticks may be inserted somewhere in the warp to help maintain the proper degree of tautness.

A silk cloth from South Sumatra, of extremely fine weaving. The warp is in stripes, with the weft pattern in real gold (not imitation) brocade.

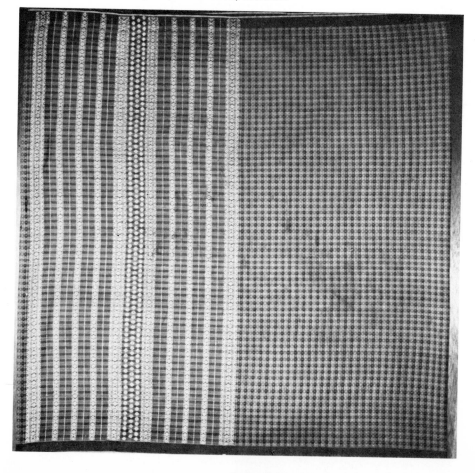

Another gold brocade, this *slendang* (scarf) is from the Padang area of North Sumatra.

A detail. The fabric is crimson cotton and silk. The brocade is real gold.

The South Sumatra *kain* in detail.

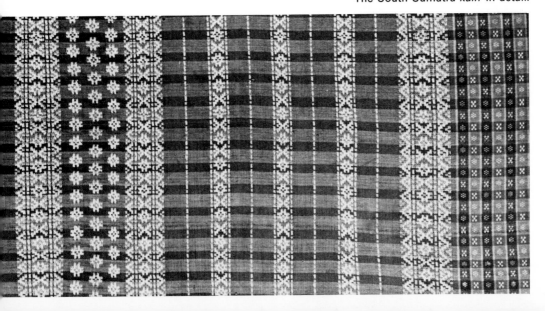

Weaving in Other Areas of Southeast Asia

Remarkable textiles are woven virtually all over Southeast Asia, sometimes using the backstrap loom, other times with more sophisticated looms that are equipped with flying shuttles and/or many harnesses. More mechanical means are also on hand in stringing the warp, in dyeing fibers, and so on. No motors are used. All operations, no matter how advanced they are mechanically, are powered by human muscles—and almost without exception by women, who are the weavers in Southeast Asia.

Brocade of silk, cotton, and gold from Muang, Lamphun (near Chiang Mai) Thailand. The pattern originated centuries ago in Laos.

Another Tausug headpiece from Jolo, the Philippines, done in a tapestry-like process.

Backstrap cotton weaving and embroidery by the Kalingas of northern Luzon, the Philippines.

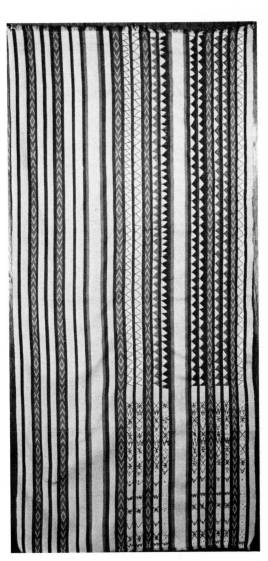

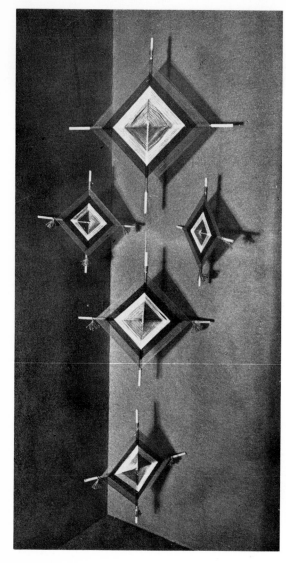

A mobile of colored cotton thread woven on cross-sticks. From Thailand.

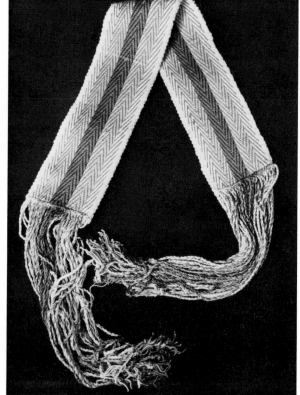

Belt made by a card-weaving process from Luzon, the Philippines.

4

PLAITING, TWINING,
AND COILING

 BACKGROUND

Plaiting, twining, and coiling are among the three most essential basket-making processes—the most common methods of working with bamboo, rattan, other palm leaves and fibers, pandanus, and various grasses found in Southeast Asia. Basketmaking (and matmaking) is woman's work. A woman often labors to create a temporary container for something; other times baskets are women's poems with the collective traditions of their lives woven into these forms. Whether art or craft, these products are short-lived because baskets are subject to all the vicissitudes of a temporal environment: mold, damage by insects, wear, excessive moisture causing rot, and fire. However, there is always another basket coming along to take its place. The basket in its various forms has lived for centuries all over the world—essentially unchanged. Plant fibers of any environment become the baskets' material. The only tool needed for basketmaking is a sharp instrument, such as a knife, and one's hands.

As we look at basket shapes and designs, it is amazing to see how continuous the design of basketry and mats appears to be. Although one sometimes can clearly identify regional styles, there are some types of plaited and coiled baskets that look as if they could come from Africa, the Americas, or from Southeast Asia. There are limits to the potential designs and what can be done with certain materials, given the process and the basket's function.

(A cross section of different types of basketry and mats is shown here.)

It is said that basketmaking developed before the potter's craft. Certainly baskets existed in Neolithic times. Few examples endured because the vegeta-

Plant fibers of any environment, such as the pandanus, surrounding Batak houses on the island of Samosir (in Lake Toba, Sumatra), become materials for making baskets.

Baskets function as hats, such as this *pis* worn by the Yakan of Basilan.
Photo Courtesy: Dottie Anderson

Dayak backpack basket from Kalimantan (the former Borneo), Indonesia.

Backpack basket from Mindanao, the Philippines.
Photo Courtesy: Dottie Anderson

Dayak basket from Sarawak.

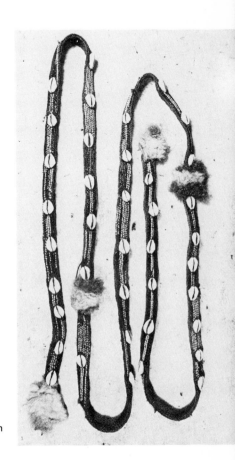

Basket from Mindanao.
Photo Courtesy: Dottie Anderson

Ikat Pinggang, a belt and shoulder harness in straw from Wamena, Irian Jaya, Indonesia.

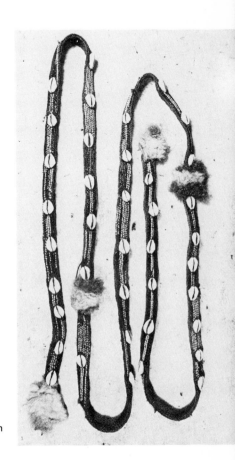

ble fibers of baskets are perishable. Looking at the scanty remains of baskets uncovered, the people of Southeast Asia are using very much the same baskets as they did millennia past.

Baskets functioned as various kinds of containers; some baskets were worn as hats, others figured as amulets to ensure a bountiful harvest, still others formed the structure of masks used in rituals; then too, the same material and process, flattened out, became roofing material, house covering, sleeping mat, and floor covering. Baskets and mats have always been inexpensive objects: plentiful, attractive, and within the reach of everyone.

A fresh palm-leaf centerpiece, called *janur*, used to celebrate special occasions by Attie Suliantoro Sulaiman. Fresh palm leaves are cut, twisted, plaited, and stitched or stapled. Sometimes a banana trunk is used as a support for the embellishments.

Woven headbands from Luzon, the Philippines.

 MATERIALS

Although basketmakers of industrial societies usually harvest their materials from catalogs, basket and mat makers of Southeast Asia reach out into their immediate environment for the materials of basketry. Grasses—hard and soft, derived from trees and plants—comprise the majority of indigenous matter. Palm, young bamboo, grasses, raffia, rattan in the form of caning, split woods, roots, stems, leaves such as pandanus, and so on are some of the basket materials. If they are stiff or hard, they are soaked before working.

Sometimes grasses and leaves are dyed by soaking or boiling with barks, fruits, and other color-yielding materials. Colors generally are subdued, in a range from golds to browns. Some people prefer the bright colors found in yarns, and dye their grasses and leaves in brilliant hues. Onionskins, ash, oak, charcoal, nutshells, tea leaves, roots of the cassava, indigo—are just some of the potential dyes to color grasses and leaves. Mordants have to be used as in any dyeing, and depending on the hardness of the material such as tough outer fibers, some substances have to soak for weeks in the dye pot in order to change their color.

Bamboo is soaked, then dried, and thin layers are split from the whole; leaves from the pandan tree (Pandanaceae family), which grows in swampy areas, are dried and then worked. Pandanus leaves (lontar palm, *Borassus flabelliforis*), which are fanlike, are also split, dried, and worked. Water is sprinkled over the worked area sometimes. Sisal (agave plants) is used for ropes and as weft materials.

Toko Mudaria and his grandson, of Bona-Gianyar, Bali, at the threshold of his rice storage loft, show me rice straw used in making ceremonial ornaments. (This area normally is visited by women.) Note the woven straw roof.

Nengah Mudaria, Toko's wife, stands before a teak tree. Leaves of the teak are used to color palm leaves dark brown.

In Bali, palm leaves are stripped into workable lengths and widths and buried underground for about four days until the palm becomes a medium brown. Some leaves are used at this stage of dyeing. Then, for a darker brown, the leaves are cooked for five or ten minutes with ground-up teak leaves (leaves from the teak tree), and then buried underground for another three or four days. The earth provides both color and mordant.

In the United States, bamboo can be found growing in the southern highlands (Tennessee, Kentucky). It has been used by the Cherokee Indians and mountain basketmakers of this area. It is hard and tough and requires soaking to render it weavable.

Splints (upright spokes of baskets) have been formed of oak, hickory, ash, birch, linden, and willow. They are cut into 1/8- to 1/2-inch widths. It is possible to beat a log with a wooden mallet, and when the fibers separate, they can be stripped with a knife or heavy shears.

Willow tips and shoots, cut in the spring or early fall, are flexible enough to weave. Cattails or rushes (varieties of *Scirpus*), gathered before they mature and dried slowly, are excellent weaving materials. The Hopi Indians of the Southwest use all parts of the yucca for spokes and for wrapping coils. Varieties of sumac (*rhu tubobata*), known as "rabbit bush," are cut in the summer, soaked, and after the bark is removed, the sapwood is cut into thin strips. This is wrapped around the rest of the twig in the coiling process. Wild honeysuckle vine should be cut in the winter, wound in rolls and boiled for four hours, soaked overnight, rinsed and dried in the sun. Grasses of various sorts should be dried in the shade slowly.

Reeds from the cane palm are imported and available in flat or rounded form in various thicknesses. And raffia, made from palm leaves, is also commonly available from suppliers.

Pandanus from Mindanao.

Leaves and water are placed in a mortar . . .

. . . and pounded with a wooden pestle.

The pulverized leaves are cooked with palm leaves
to create the brown color.

Various shades of palm leaf from beige to brown.

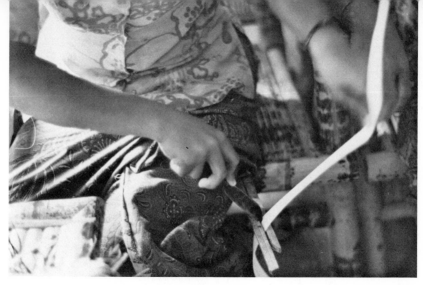

Two strips of bamboo are lashed together, closely enough to draw the palm leaf through. The point of a knife cuts the palm leaf as the leaf is pulled through slit.

TOOLS AND EQUIPMENT

Since many of these materials have to be flexible to use, they have to be soaked beforehand. Therefore, a water supply must be at hand.

Some device such as shears or knives is used for cutting the materials into proper working lengths. And an awl, knitting or darning needle, or some kind of pointed instrument is handy to poke holes or generally facilitate weaving. Sometimes pliers come in handy to pull through difficult lengths. Note the device used to split palm leaf—two strips of bamboo, lashed closely together, just enough to pull the palm leaf through, and the point of a knife, held at a fixed point, while the leaf is being drawn through the slit.

CONSTRUCTION PROCESSES

Coiling

Coiling was probably one of the earliest methods of basketmaking. It is similar to making coiled pottery. In coiled work, stiff bundles of grasses or similar materials are wrapped in a spiral and, as they are coiled, stitched together in various ways, as described in the diagram. Some kind of pointed instrument is used to spread open a hole so that a soft grass or leaflike material can be inserted to bind one coil to the other with a stitch or loop. Often the stiffer coil material requires soaking before coiling easily. And if different colors are to be used for binding and wrapping the coils, these require dyeing beforehand.

Shapes and sizes can be controlled by how the coils are stacked or revolved. If they are allowed to grow larger in circumference than the previous coil, the shape will expand; conversely, smaller coils will reduce the size.

In some pieces, such as the Philippine basket shown here, coiling is modified by employing a knot stitch. The essential structure grows by coiling, in this case into an oval shape. Each coil is attached to the other by looping fibers around bottom and top coil and making a knot between the coil and around the loops.

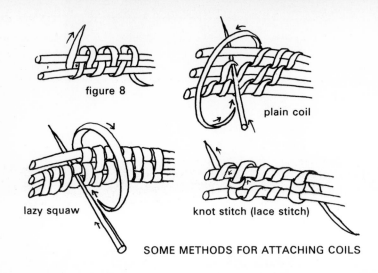

figure 8

plain coil

lazy squaw

knot stitch (lace stitch)

SOME METHODS FOR ATTACHING COILS

A coconut shell woven into a base, constructed in essentially a lazy squaw stitch. By the Toradjas of Sulawesi.

Sukong, a Bontoc man's hat (Luzon, the Philippines). The Bontoc man stores his pipe and tobacco inside it.

Lady's purse in knot stitch from Leyte, the Philippines.

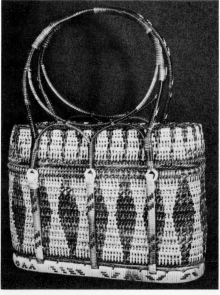

pplementary warp ikat from Sumba, Indonesia.

Hudok mask from Longiram district, up the Mahakam River in Kalimantan (Borneo), Indonesia.

Lokub containers uniquely made by the Maranao of Mindanao, the Philippines.

Wedding sarong embroidered in gold by couching. From Lampong district Sumatra, Indonesia.

Maranao Lutuan, silver inlay in bronze, betel nut box cast in the lost wax process. From near Marawi, Mindanao, the Philippines.

Porcelain from Thailand.

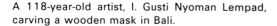

A 118-year-old artist, I. Gusti Nyoman Lempad, carving a wooden mask in Bali.

Extremely fine seed bead necklace. Dayak from Kalimantan, Indonesia.

Terra-cotta sculpture from Kasongan, Java, Indonesia.

Betel nut set. Lacquer over fibers, sgraffito design, repoussé silver containers. Cambodia.

Ancestor figure, possibly from Amanamkai village on the As River in the Asmat area of Irian Jaya, Indonesia (near New Guinea).

Section of a carved and polychromed Batak house front, near Lake Toba, North Sumatra.

Reverse appliqué, appliqué, and embroidery of the Meo people, northern Thailand.

Close-up of a *langkit,* a strip of inlay weaving decoratively used to join other woven areas to create the tubular *malong* dress of the Maranao woman From Marawi, Mindanao, the Philippines.

Vegetable fiber vest in a tightly braided and knitted technique. From Irian Jaya.

Papier-mâché dance mask from Chiang Mai, Thailand.

Hand-carved stone entranceway to a temple. Bali.

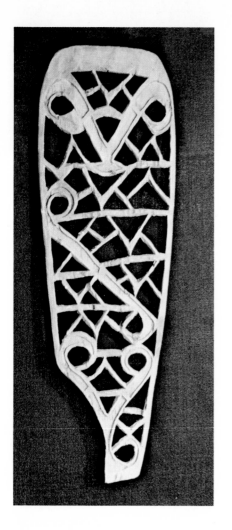

Carved wooden paddle head from Irian Jaya, Indonesia.

Plaited palm leaf, polychromed basket from Sarawak.

T'boli bead belt with lost wax cast-bronze bells. From Mindanao, the Philippines.

Palm-leaf rice offering figure from Bali, Indonesia.

Carved wooden ancestor figure with inlaid ivory teeth and eyes. Possibly from Flores, Indonesia.

Contemporary Balinese art painting of a traditional ceremony.

The remarkable double ikat of Tenganan, Bali. Called *geringsing,* it takes many years to weave.

Plaited pandanus-leaf hanging from eastern Sanur, the Philippines.

Traditional batik from Java, Indonesia.

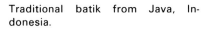

An old coil tray made in knot stitch. From Sulawesi.

Pandanus basket in knot stitch from southern Kalimantan.

Another coiling variation found in Balacca, Sulawesi (Indonesia), are baskets made of palm leaves that have been dyed in bright (aniline) colors to match bright colored sarongs. These containers are used to hold food, cosmetics, etc.

Dyed palm leaves are split to the proper width with a razor set in wood, and cardboard is used as a width guide. The center of the palm leaf, which is thicker and stiffer, is used to form individual rings. Then the strips of palm leaf are crossed over top and bottom rings using a figure 8.

The basket can be shaped by increasing or decreasing the size of the rings. Sometimes details are woven through the vertically wrapped fibers, as if they were a warp, using different colors of "weft" to create design variations on the side, bottom, and for the handle of the lid.

Making a Buginese basket in Balacca, Sulawesi. Palm leaf and the center spine of the leaf are used in constructing this basket. The center spine is moistened and wrapped around this cylinder to help form a circle.

Overlapping ends are thinned with a knife to help maintain an even thickness as ends overlap.

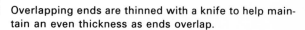

Palm leaves are sliced to an even width using a razor blade set in bamboo.

The coil is rolled to the proper diameter . . .

. . . and set into the previous coils. Wider diameters create wider openings with narrower diameters reducing the circumference.

With a flexible palm leaf, the figure 8 coiling stitch . . .

. . . is used to attach the more rigid spine to previous coils.

The stitch loops around two coils and then one coil, alternating around the basket.

Two completed baskets.

Plaiting Mats

Plaiting is weaving without a loom and is probably the most common process for making containers, fences, and mats. A wide range of shapes and designs is possible with plaiting. The materials of the tropics—pandanus, lontar palm leaves, and so forth—are plentiful, the tools simple. The products are handsome. And because of this, plaiting is practiced in many parts of Southeast Asia from the Philippines to Indonesia. To the Samaloan people of Rio Hondo, near Zamboanga, Mindanao (Philippines), the Menangkabau in Central Sumatra (Indonesia), and the Dayaks of Kalimantan (Indonesia), plaiting plays an important part in family life.

Traditionally, mats were used only for sleeping. Now they are made into shopping bags, place mats, and wall hangings. The old designs, along with new symbols, are plaited into these forms.

Essentially, pandanus leaves, lontar palm leaves, and sometimes grasses are used for plaiting. Leaves are dried, stripped, boiled, and dyed with aniline colors. They are again dried and bundled, ready for plaiting. The only other material needed is a knife. Sometimes stones are used to hold down groups of strands.

THREE STEPS TO BEGIN PLAITING

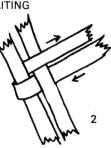
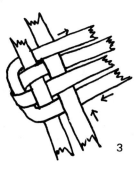

1

2

3

Very beautiful pandanus mats are plaited by the Samaloans of Rio Hondo near Zamboanga, Mindanao. The leaves are dried, stripped, boiled, and dyed with aniline colors. Then they are dried, bundled, and plaited into mats.

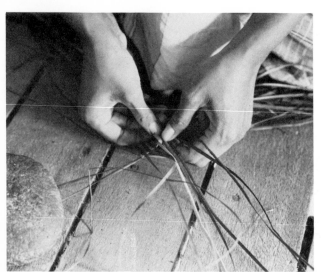

Most of the patterns are plaited as shown here, on a diagonal.

Designs vary considerably. About twelve dextral lengths are woven at the same time.

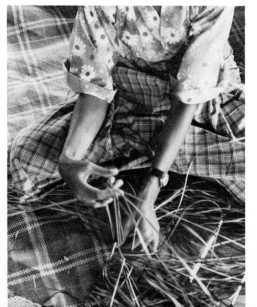

Plaiting design for mats is usually formed in diagonal directions in Southeast Asia, with small and large plaids quite common. Large mural forms, used for wall hangings, are a decorative mutation.

The leaves just prior to weaving are often beaten with a stick to soften them and then they are rolled around fingers or a stick to make them more pliable. The general procedure for weaving is to start in the left corner, establish one side and the bottom edge, increase the number of wefts along the bottom edge and complete the right corner, then complete the left corner and finish the top edge, tucking away weft ends until the right top corner has been formed. The last two strands are woven back into the corner. Work is built up in small sections, which then can be joined to wider sections or be widened. There are two identical wefts—the *dextral* and the *sinistral* (to distinguish between the two), which are plaited one under and over the other. Usually ten dextrals are worked at one time. This is about as many as can be plaited comfortably. New wefts are added as needed to extend the old wefts as they become too short. Old and new wefts are overlapped for about an inch, then the old wefts are dropped (and cut off later). In plaiting a plain mat, the bottom and top edges are dominated by dextrals and the side edges are formed by the right angle turns of sinistrals. Patterns are created by adding dextral and sinistral wefts at predetermined points. Other variations are achieved by weaving over two and under one at certain points—much like in weaving on a loom. The diagrams and photos shown here describe the basic steps in plaiting flat surfaces.

One of the many mat patterns of the Samaloans. Some designs are traditional, others new.

A colorful "parrot" mat plaited in eastern Sanur, the Philippines.

A long (six-foot) sleeping mat with a plain plaited lining. This traditional Samaloan pattern is called Sico, meaning elbow.

Plaiting Ornaments

Plaiting ornaments follows the same basic principles but applies them in three dimensions. The strands of grass or leaves are folded, turned, and sometimes twisted to create the effects as shown by the Thai boy who is plaiting a simple star from palm leaf. These materials are lightweight and therefore can be strung, hung, and used for holiday ornamentation.

There is a long tradition of plaiting ornaments. This lad from northern Thailand is soaking pandanus in water to impart flexibility to the fibers.

First steps in plaiting.

Lengths are woven through again and folded in diagonal points.

Excess is cut away with scissors.

The finished star sits among the materials for creating more ornaments.

Plaited pandanus ornaments are found throughout Southeast Asia. This mobile is hung during celebrations by the Buginese in Sulawesi.

Plaiting Baskets

Plaiting is probably the most popular basketmaking process in Southeast Asia. Just as in matmaking, very beautiful patterns emerge when different colors of grasses or leaves are used. Shapes vary as well in a range of three-dimensional forms from rectangular boxes with lids to envelope shapes, carrying baskets to be worn on one's back, trays, and ceremonial offering baskets.

Usually plaiting results in a flexible, yielding material that gives when weight is pressed against the plaited surface; therefore, a support system is necessary. The only exception is when stiffer, more rigid bamboo or rattan is used. Very often support is supplied by a decorative skeletal structure of a stiffer material that is lashed to the outside of the basket. Other times, the basket form is mounted on a rigid base (often of bamboo or rattan) or the basket is lined with another reinforcing layer of the same plaited material.

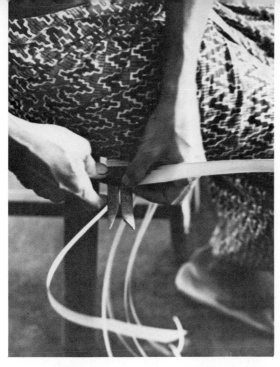

Palm leaves are cut to the desired width.

Nengah Mudaria plaits a flat surface.

Before bending the form, leaves are moistened . . .

... and corners are bent in a diagonal.

Lengths that meet are woven together.

A miniaturized version in multiples.

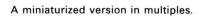

A nest of lidded baskets from the Philippines. A nest of baskets from the Philippines, made rigid by a rigid rattan base.

When a basket has a lid that slides over the base, as a slipcase, this second lid form provides that extra bit of necessary support. Plaited baskets have to be designed with the reinforcing method becoming an integral part of the shape. Unlike coiled, twined, or woven baskets, there are no vertical splines or stakes to maintain their shape. But because of this, the range of potential form is broader and more varied with a container having no gaps, holes, or seams.

Baskets made of wide elements usually have simple patterns or have no designs. In order to achieve a variety of pattern, the weaving elements have to be finer. Most often, some of the leaves are dyed a darker brown, while others are left their natural tan color.

The type of design is determined by the width of the wefts, the system of plaiting, and the number of colors introduced. Basic plaiting is over one, under one. With this structure, bands, stripes, checks, or plaids are possible. To vary the design pattern, deviation from over one, under one, to floating wefts over two or three and under one or more, results in a wide range of patterns. If the floating extends much beyond over three, things tend to catch on the surface and the basket is vulnerable to tearing.

A plaited basket from Jogjakarta, Java. This design appears throughout Asia.

A wooden X shape supports this plaited basket from Chiang Rai, Thailand.

A plaited palm-leaf slipcase is being finished off. From Bona-Giangar, Bali.

Two very old slipcases from Bali. Forms such as these are used to store papers, pictures, and other flat valuables.

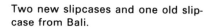

Two new slipcases and one old slipcase from Bali.

Sewn Forms

Broad widths of leaves, usually pandanus or palm, have been made into head and food covers. Leaves are overlapped and stitched together with cotton threads. Sometimes spines of palm leaves are used to form the ribbing or a structural support for the hat or food cover. The stitching, sometimes combined with sequins and/or beads, adds a decorative surface touch to the cover. Often the stitches form an embroidered pattern as well as a network to keep the leaves from tearing.

A sewn palm hat from the Philippines.

Palm-leaf temple and festival ornaments are made in Bali to pay homage to the gods and to ensure a good harvest.

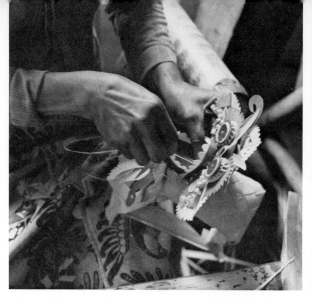

Here is Rangda again, made of palm leaf this time.

The completed colorful Rangda mask from Bali.

A lamak offering made of cut and sewn palm leaf. Offerings such as these, in pairs that represent male and female, are created as a gesture of reverence to the deities.

A palm-leaf hat from Mindanao.

Note the fine and precise stitching that holds the fine circular ribs onto the flat leaves.

An old teak-dyed pandanus food-cover basket, about 18 inches in diameter. Designs are embroidered with colored thread (the same thread that stitches the leaves together) and sequins. From Bali.

Twined and Woven Baskets

Twined and woven baskets are also made in Southeast Asia. Often these containers are lined with plaited pandanus or palm. Except for one rare piece, found in Bagio, Luzon (the Philippines), that was twined of brass and copper wire, the materials for these baskets are usually the more rigid rattan or bamboo.

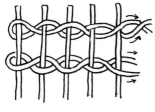

Twining

Weaving

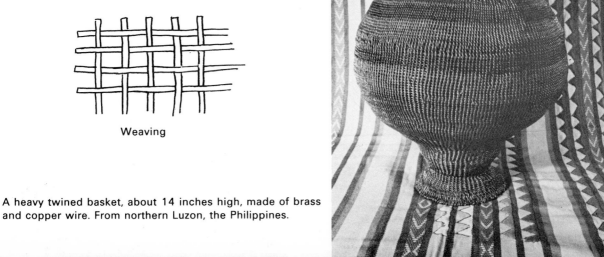

A heavy twined basket, about 14 inches high, made of brass and copper wire. From northern Luzon, the Philippines.

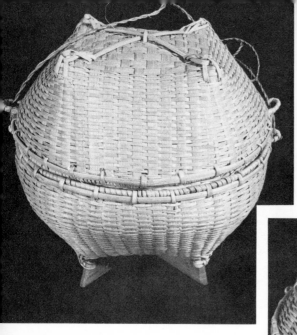

A woven bamboo basket on a wooden X base from Chiang Mai, Thailand.

Note that this basket sports a plaited bamboo liner.

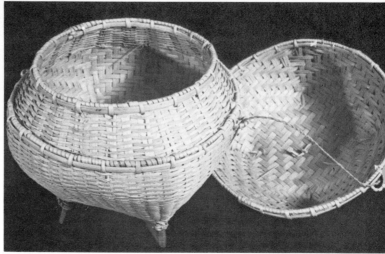

An unusual brown, beige, and yellow striped fiber vest in a braided and knitted technique. Pieces of animal fur are sewn on in places. From Irian Jaya.

A collection of old Akha hill-tribe woven baskets, all with plaited liners. From Kaw Saen Chai, northwest of Chiang Rai, near the Burma border.

5

BAMBOO AND LACQUER

 BAMBOO

Bamboo has touched the daily lives of the people of Southeast Asia in numerous, vital ways from providing the material for containers, thatch for roofs, walls of houses, mats for floors, windshield and barrier for flooding, to weapons, pipes, instruments, food, medicine, sieves, stakes, bridges, brooms, and so on—it is one of the most useful plants known.

Bamboo is extraordinary in other ways. It flowers once in more or less a hundred years and then dies. It can complete its growing in two months and then remain the same size for the rest of its life. Bamboo grows so fast it is sometimes possible to observe green stems growing in the spring. Indeed bamboo is unique; not a tree, it is often indicated as a grass and also as a kind of rice. Whatever, bamboo is characterized by its *culm,* which is the stem or trunk that has joints and is hollow; by large and small roots and rhizomes that quickly grow underground, alternating in growth periods with the culm, and shooting up new sprouts that grow into new culms. Most bamboo usually grows in clumps in the tropics, grouped together because it likes some shade. The diameter of bamboo varies from 0.1 inch to 7 inches, and its height as well, from 1 foot to 60 feet. There are over a thousand varieties of bamboo —at least 1,250 species and 50 genera. Some are grown for eating (bamboo shoots), others for the many specific uses for bamboo. Because the growth cycle of bamboo is completed in about a year, harvesting can be programmed usually in five- or six-year cycles. Bamboo that is young is too soft for most craft purposes, while older plants are too hard and become prone to insect infestation.

A set of bamboo baskets, one nesting into the other. From northern Luzon, the Philippines.

A T'boli woman carrying water in bamboo tubes.
Photo Courtesy: Dottie Anderson

A stand of bamboo and a close-up showing a culm and leaves.
Drawing by Dionisio G. Orellana

Stacks of bamboo drying in the sun.

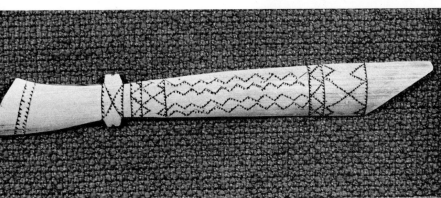

In some parts of Southeast Asia, a bamboo knife is used to cut the umbilical cord of a newborn baby. This is not a knife but a nit-picker of the T'boli.

Most species of bamboo like warm weather, but there are some kinds that can survive below freezing (such as black kurockiku from Japan).*

Because bamboo has been for so long a part of the cultural history of the East, there is much lore attached to bamboo. For instance, it is believed that cutting the umbilical cord of a newly born baby should be performed with a bamboo knife—for a girl, a knife made from male bamboo and for a boy, one from female bamboo.

It is not uncommon, while driving through the countryside of Southeast Asian countries, to see stacks of bamboo drying in the sun, waiting for the proper moment for cutting, splitting, or whatever purpose the bamboo is to serve.

Uses

One common use for bamboo, as indicated earlier in Chapter 4, is for basketmaking. Another is for mat weaving, both for floors and the sides of houses. In fact, entire houses are constructed of bamboo—an available, inexpensive, and practical material for the tropics. Bamboo has been used for building furniture, fashioning tools, as covers for the traditional venetian-blind-like book of Southeast Asia (pages are of palm leaf), and significantly, for the creating of all kinds of containers.

*For those who are interested in growing bamboo, a beautiful book entitled *Bamboo,* by Robert Austin, Dana Levy, and Koichiro Ueda (Tokyo and New York: Weatherhill, 1972), describes all aspects of bamboo.

Matmaking in Sulawesi. The Buginese use woven bamboo for covering the walls of their houses.

Strips of bamboo are woven over three, under three, in a "twill" pattern.

A knife is pounded against each weft to close gaps between the newly woven strip and the last woven piece.

Very large pieces are woven using these stiff slices of bamboo. Note the rolls of bamboo in the background.

One of various woven designs on a Sulawesi house near Sengkang.

Another Sulawesi house sporting woven bamboo walls.

Lee Newman gets a lesson in operating a bamboo bow drill. Note the bamboo furniture to the right. This drill is still being used to drill holes. Interestingly, this same type of drill has been used until recently by American Indians of the Southwest.

A bamboo arrow and arrow case.

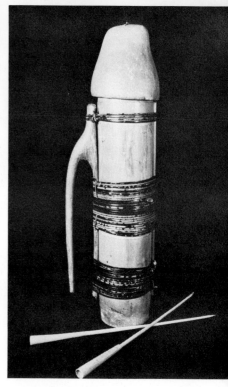

Toko Mudaria with reading glasses, opening an ancient bamboo-covered book with inscriptions on palm leaf pages. Note, in contrast, the Western-style book sitting beneath it.

A bamboo Dayak arrow case from central Kalimantan.

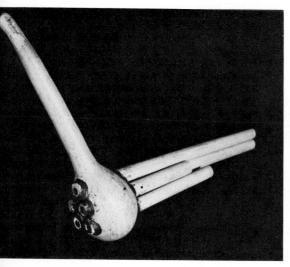

Now called a document container, it is used for many items from knitting needles to arrows. By the Toradjas, central Sulawesi. Designs are burned in and colored. (*below left*).

An ancient Batak bamboo medicine container with a carved wooden stopper from the Prapat area of Sumatra. (*below right*).

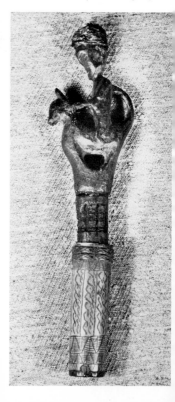

A flute-like instrument of bamboo and gourd, sealed where they join with pitch. Called a *kaen,* it is played by the Akha, hill-tribe people of Thailand. The Dayaks of Sarawak have a similar instrument that they call a *kledi.*

A Batak amulet from Samosir Island, Lake Toba, Sumatra.

On the right, a contemporary Batak container with a calendar scratched around the bamboo tube. The bamboo on the left contains symbolic designs.

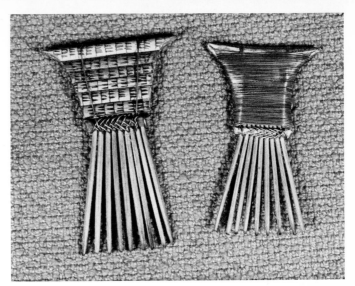

T'boli hair combs of bamboo and brass wire. Designs are burned into the comb (*on the left*).

A bamboo tray made by the Toradjas of central Sulawesi. Strips of bamboo are slid into grooves of the frame around the tray. No adhesive is used.

Decoration

The surface of bamboo lends itself to several different decorative techniques. Using a sharply pointed instrument, the hard bamboo outer layer can be scratched and then filled in with color. This is perhaps the most universal approach to decorating bamboo. Another method is to burn in the design. And a unique process, seen only in the Lake Lanao area of Mindanao, is the Lokub-making process illustrated here.*

"Lokub" is a Maranao word for the bamboo tube used for stacking or processing chewing tobacco for a more flavorful taste. The container caught the fancies of the local artisans and they embellished these forms by decorating the surface all around. The earliest attempts were made by scratching geometric and curved lines with a sharply pointed pocketknife; or by burning lines and filling them with coconut shell umber. This was men's work. The designs we see today are a relatively new process that emerged somewhere during the middle of the nineteenth century.

"Lakusan," a local Maranao term, refers to wrapping. In the little town of Inudaran, located along the shores of Lake Lanao, 11 kilometers south of Marawi City, Mindanao, lokub-making has become a central craft of the people. It has been believed that lokub-a-lakusan originated in this town.

One important factor to consider for making successful lokubs is the type of bamboo used. "Tring" is the local name; *Bambusa blumeneana* -Schultes F. is the botanical term. This particular bamboo has a semiglossy appearance, is smooth to the touch, and has a longer culm space than most varieties—from 14 to 18 inches apart. The diameter ranges from 3 to 4 inches with a wall thickness of 1/4 to 5/8 of an inch; this does not include the spacing of the basal and the near portion of the tip. The whole bamboo tree looks slim against the blue sky, growing 90 feet or more in height.

In determining the right type of bamboo for lokub-making, skill and experience are necessary in order to select the bamboo at the proper growing point. But more is involved than that; Maranao bamboo cutters are superstitious. They cut bamboo on moonless nights because they believe that in doing so, their bamboo will not be susceptible to pinhole insects such as powder-post beetles.

Although the design of bamboo lokub was conceived during the height of the betel nut, pepper leaf, and tobacco chewing days, the lokub is still being made, even though the Maranao people, for the most part, have stopped chewing. Now the lokub is created not as a tobacco container but for tourist and local use as flower vases and pencil holders, to name a few.

Bamboo lokub-a-lakusan is a joint male and female operation. Selecting, cutting, scraping, and trimming are performed by men. Gathering of fuel, cooking, purchasing of materials needed such as dye, manila paper, etc., are also done by men. The cutout designs, coloring, pasting, tying and wrapping using banana leaves, and the rinsing are performed by women. With betel nut's flesh, the polishing may be executed by either women or men. Then, the selling and pricing of the lokub is considered a man's job.

---

*This process is shown in line drawings made by Dionisio G. Orellana of Iligan City (the Philippines). A revolt in the area made it impossible for me to photograph the process.

A priest-scribe from Tenganan, Bali, scratches a story onto a palm leaf of a bamboo book. Note the swastika, called a *bandji*. This is an ancient motif in Southeast Asia, which was said to have been introduced there from China. It is a magic sign of good fortune and prosperity. He is using the tip of a magnificent gold-adorned carved wooden *kris* (knife).

The scribe rubs coloring from the fruit of a tree into the scratches.

Two illustrated books, one closed, the other open. Illustrations are extremely fine. An ancient coin keeps the cord from slipping out.

A close-up map delineating the area around Lake Lanao where the Maranao lokubs are made.

Almost all Maranao women have knowledge of weaving. They are taught to weave from a very early age. Their weaving designs are essentially geometric. This has influenced the designs and colors seen on the lokub. If you study the designs on the lokubs shown here and look at the langkit (vertical) and tubiran, which is the horizontal narrow strip weaving sewn in the malong (Chapter 4), you will see great similarity.

After "middle-aged" bamboo is cut at the proper point, the excess culm that protrudes is cut away, in alternating directions, once wielding a knife toward one end, and another time in the opposite direction.

A *nawi* (knife) is used to scrape off the hard outer layer to reveal the woody section and an ocher-colored grain.

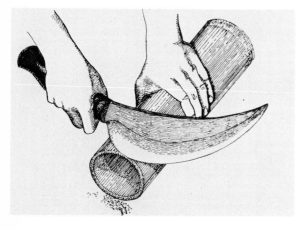

The length to be cut is measured with hand lengths to determine a somewhat standard one-foot length. Then the rim is cut as one hand rotates the bamboo against the knife blade.

Supplies are gathered. *At the top,* a *papag*—a wooden basin usually used as a mixing bowl in cakemaking; *below it,* an enameled basin; *to the right,* a gasoline can with top cut off; *center:* a sheet of manila paper or heavy kraft paper; *lower left to right,* string, starch, Chinese dye, *loguitip,* a sandpaper-like leaf; *bottom,* freshly cut banana leaves.

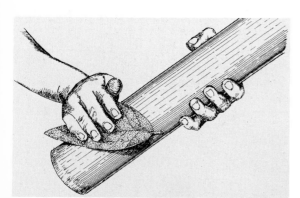

The bamboo surface is sanded to smooth finish with the loguitip, sandpaper-textured leaves.

Chinese dye is dissolved in cold water and is rubbed on a piece of manila paper by hand.

Cotton crochet thread is soaked in a basin of dye.

Several colors of the now dyed manila paper are placed on banana leaves for drying in the sun, along with dyed string.

Designs are cut by women, both with a pocket-knife and with scissors. For discontinuous shapes, pieces of dyed paper are folded and cut.

The geometric colored shapes are pasted directly onto the bamboo with the dyed side of the paper in contact with the bamboo surface. The paste is made by cooking cornstarch with water, stirring constantly to avoid lumps.

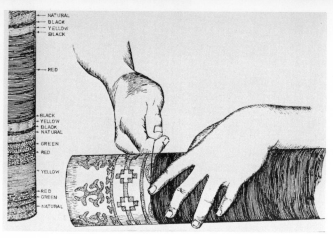

The dyed string is wound tightly and closely together around the entire bamboo, covering paper-decorated and undecorated areas as well. Various colors of string may be used. Each end is tucked under the next winding. Care is taken not to dislocate the pasted cutout designs.

The entire tube is wrapped in banana leaves and tied securely with string.

All the wrapped tubes that can be accommodated in a petroleum can are placed vertically in the can, which is then filled with water. Cooking commences.

After boiling for several minutes, a piece of tube is pulled out, partway, to check whether color has transferred at that point. Color transfer can be seen around the culm rim, if it has penetrated.

The pieces are removed; banana leaf wrappers are untied, and the piece is rinsed until all excess color has been washed away.

All tubes are then polished with young betel nut meat, which serves as a varnish . . .

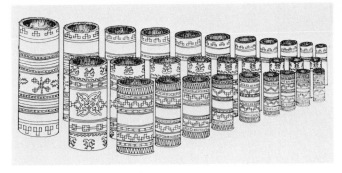

... and the pieces are left to dry in the shade.

Two completed lokubs from Mindanao.

Three other designs. The center one is old, and somewhat faded. Each design has its own name.

Lokub-making is essentially a paper-cutting and dyeing process that results in colorful patterns. A practical approach, far less complicated than the Lanao del Sur process, is to cut designs from the variety of colorful tissue paper or crepe paper that easily bleeds its color when wet. After sanding the bamboo, wrap the bamboo surface with the cut designs of tissue paper, then moisten the paper with a wet sponge. This will cause a transfer of a colored dye pattern to the bamboo. The brilliant colors can be applied (similar to the paper-cutout technique of the Lanao lokub) in a progression of colors repeating in a striped design.

 LACQUERWARE

Lacquerware has long been famous in China and Japan, but rarely credited to Southeast Asia, where it also is an art form. Examples of lacquerware dating back to the second century B.C. were discovered in a former Han-dynasty tomb in Hunan Province, China. In Burma and Thailand, the art has been developed in a very different approach. Both countries share a common heritage, inasmuch as the art probably originated in China. Although wood has been used traditionally as a base for some lacquer pieces, straw or horsehair is also employed.

Lacquer has been applied to architectural components on a grand scale, in concert with gold leaf, to furniture and to small objects designed for both personal and monastic use. For larger forms, lacquer is applied much like paint to a surface. Small objects are made of wood or very finely woven or plaited bamboo or of plaited horsehair. The interstices of the basketlike form are filled and the entire piece is lacquered many times. Sometimes different colors of lacquer are brushed on, one over the other, and then designs are scraped through to the various layers of color; other times work is restricted to black and gold.

The lacquer material itself varies from place to place. Generally it is a natural resin of some kind—animal or plant. One animal secretion, *lac*, resembles plant resins in many aspects. The lac-producing insect, *Coccus lacca*, is indigenous to India. Larvae of the insects secrete lac around themselves and the twig on which they are attached, providing a protective coating. Twigs are gathered and the stick lac is removed and purified by boiling in water. The resulting product that is skimmed off is shellac, and *not lacquer*. The lacquer material used in most of Southeast Asia is gathered from the sap of the sumac tree or the *thitsi* tree. Contrary to the dry atmosphere necessary for the application of shellac, lacquer dries best in a very humid, hot atmosphere.

The compound of the Grand Palace in Bangkok, Thailand, houses many buildings and temples that are elegantly decorated with lacquer in various colors and in gold leaf.

One of the guardians of the Wat Phra Keo of the Grand Palace in Bangkok. The entire towering sculpture is covered in lacquer and gold leaf.

A miniature lidded container in lacquer and gold leaf.

The Process

The process varies somewhat from place to place, but generally methods fall into two categories—lacquer is applied over a seasoned, grainless, lightweight wood such as wood from the banyan tree, or over a woven or plaited form made of bamboo or horsehair.

ON WOOD

If wood is used, the wood is well seasoned (at least a year) and is a grainless type with very little resin. Wood from the linden tree, or wood from the birch family, is desirable. The wood is turned into the desired shape on a lathe, or the form is constructed. Before lacquering, in some places, a base coat of camellia oil (or linseed oil can be used), pig's blood, and blue clay is applied to the piece in order to seal the wood. (A wood sealer compatible with lacquer can also be employed.) The pig's blood is said to "strengthen" the wood and prevent cracking later. It actually acts as a binder or adhesive for the oil and clay.

Three to six coats of strained lacquer are then applied by brush, allowing each coat to dry thoroughly in a humid, hot, dust-free atmosphere. Between each coating of lacquer, the piece is rubbed with a pumice stone and a "sandpaper" leaf until a smooth surface is achieved.

ON WOVEN OR PLAITED FORMS

Finely woven bamboo baskets provide a fine lightweight base for lacquerware. The basket is woven while the bamboo is wet. After the proper size has been achieved, the top is coated with a bitumen- or pitchlike material that acts as an adhesive to keep the topmost weaving from fraying. The excess spokes are cut away when the adhesive has cured.

The interstices of the basket now need to be filled. The same bitumen- or pitch-like material is used. When the filler material has dried, the piece is turned on a lathe to create even thicknesses in the walls of the container.

Making a lacquer bowl involves a great many processes and stages as seen here—from the fibers on the left all the way to the lacquering.

Woven reed bowls, waiting for the lacquer process, are the foundation for lacquerware from Thailand.

Bamboo spokes and finely stripped reed are used in bowl-weaving.

Weaving reed around bamboo spokes.

The bowl before painting the edge with bitumen to seal it and prior to trimming excess lengths of spokes.

Pitch, or bitumen, is used to fill the interstices of the basket. On the right, the piece has been turned on a lathe.

Then a mixture of powdered charcoal and soy is applied. No doubt the soy acts as the adhesive or binder for the powdered charcoal. When this coating dries, it is sanded smooth and the applications of strained black (dirt-free) lacquer begin. Sometimes the lacquer is brushed on, other times it is applied with a flexible spatula while the form is slowly rotated.

After each of the three to six coatings dries, the vessel is sanded until the surface is smooth and even. Sometimes the lacquer is sanded while the bowl is turned on the lathe.

A scene showing the lathe and area for turning.

A bowl being turned on a lathe, inside surface first . . .

. . . then outside.

After turning (*on the left*), a mixture of powdered charcoal and soy is applied, resulting in the finish on the right.

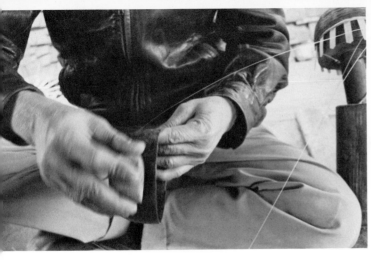

When this coating dries, it is sanded to a smooth finish.

The lacquer is strained.   Many coats of lacquer are applied . . .

. . . sometimes with a spatula, as shown here, and sometimes with a brush.

After each of three to six coatings has dried, the vessel is wet-sanded on a lathe until it is smooth and even.

Various stages of decorating the completed bowl, seen from right to left.

A completed black lacquer bowl, with gold-leaf decoration. From Chiang Mai, Thailand.

An orange lacquer betel nut set coated over reed or horsehair, from Burma. The design is scratched through to a layer of black and green.

The set contains several small compartments in two trays. The silver repoussé receptacles were used for lime and other components used in betel nut chewing ceremonies.

Decorating the Surface

There are many different approaches to decorating the lacquered surface. One simple method is to scratch a design into the lacquer. Then, with a waxy metallic stick (much like Rub'n Buf in consistency), the waxy metallic color is rubbed and pressed into the scratches. Excess is wiped away and the surface is buffed clean of excess color. The metallic filler only remains in the scratches, filling them.

Another approach is to paint on designs directly with metallic-colored (usually gold or silver) lacquer.

A different process, one that is more traditional, is to apply gold leaf to the lacquered surface. To do this, the design is demarcated on the black lacquer by pounding a chalk-filled cotton sack over tissue paper that had been pricked into a pinhole design with a pin. The chalk sifts through these holes as white linear deposits of chalk on the black lacquered surface.

All the negative spaces, not to be gold leafed, are painted with a water and vinegar mixture. This serves as a mask. Then water-free lacquer is rubbed with a cotton ball over the area to be gold leafed. The gold leafing is placed gingerly over the lacquer, which acts as an adhesive. After a few moments, with powder-coated fingers, gold leaf is pressed on the surface, adhering it to the lacquer. Powdered fingers keep the gold leaf from pulling away from the surface as usually only fingers touch the leaf.

Next, the entire piece is placed in water, is allowed to soak for a little while, and when sitting in water, excess gold leaf is rubbed away wherever the water-soluble mask of water and vinegar had been applied earlier. The result is a gold-leafed design, as smoothly applied as the lacquer surface itself.

With an awl, a line design is scratched into the lacquered surface.

A waxy gold metallic stick is rubbed over the scratches filling them in.

The excess is wiped away.

And the surface is buffed with a soft cheesecloth.

Yet another lacquer decorating technique is accomplished by scratching through successive layers of lacquer to reveal the color beneath. At each depth another color appears, depending, of course, on how many colors were applied in the first place.

Tissue paper that has a design pinpricked into it is placed on a lacquered bowl and a pack of chalk is pounded over the surface . . .

. . . leaving a deposit through the holes, as an outline of the design.

All the negative spaces, not to be gold-leafed, are painted with a water and vinegar (acetic acid) mixture. This serves as a mask.

Water-free lacquer is rubbed with a cotton ball over the surface, and gold leafing is placed gingerly over the sticky lacquer.

With powder-coated fingers, the gold leaf is pressed onto the surface, adhering it to the lacquer.

The entire piece is placed in water, allowed to soak for a few minutes . . .

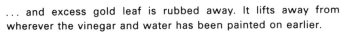

. . . and excess gold leaf is rubbed away. It lifts away from wherever the vinegar and water has been painted on earlier.

6

CARVING: WOOD, STONE, AND IVORY

 BACKGROUND AND LORE

Wood carving existed in Neolithic times. Small stone adzes and axes used for shaping wood have been uncovered. They were small enough to indicate that wood carvings exhibited delicate details. The stone ax and adze were around for a long time, just recently (since World War II) replaced by metal adzes in West Irian (Irian Jaya), particularly in the Asmat area. Wood carving is a vigorous art—requiring vigor in cutting and resulting in dynamic form.

Wood (or stone) as sculpture closely relates to social custom and religious concepts. It is a three-dimensional rendering of fantasy thinking. Spirits are thought to reside in carved wooden figures and they are alleged to carry supernatural powers. Ancestor figures appeared throughout the Indonesian Archipelago and are carved there to this day. People also had built elaborate temples, complete with figures, of their dead kings. (The king was thought of as an incarnation of God on earth.) The Buddhists brought their stone carvings of Buddha and the various bodhisattvas; the Hindus created carvings of Brahma, Vishnu, and Shiva—and these newer forms resided side by side with the original ancestor figures. Where else were the spirits of ancestors going to live?

In Thailand there are spirit houses, and something similar to the ubiquitous spirit house can also be seen in the home compound of the Balinese. Ancestor figures are being carved today in the Batak areas of Sumatra, in Nias and in Kalimantan by the Dayaks and in the northern section of Luzon in the Philippines.

The old ancestor forms were well accommodated by Buddhists and Hindus. But when Islam came to Java, wood and stone carving of images stopped.

Until comparatively recently, in many parts of Southeast Asia, carving was accomplished via a stone ax, such as this one.

Spirit houses, small temples to the ubiquitous spirit, are in every family compound in Bali. The vase sitting on Nengah Mudaria's head is an offering.

Offerings and straw ornaments, gifts of goodwill, are placed in the niche of the carved stone spirit house. From Bali.

Ancestor figures, Dayak from Sarawak.

Dayak ancestor figures from Kalimantan are about two inches high and carved of hardwoods. Usually, these figures are linked together with weavings of bamboo, beads, or some kind of string.

Dayak hampatong figures from Kalimantan to ward off evil spirits. Curiously, this figure is carrying a dog on his back, and emerging from a sack upon which the dog is standing is the head of another person.

An Igorot ancestor figure on a bracelet that is made of a pair of tusks. Northern Luzon, Philippines.

A *bihang* is a savage and devil-like idol of the Ifugao (Luzon, the Philippines). Fear is generated by its presence and powers, enough to inflict bad luck on lawbreakers.

On the other hand, a *bulol* is a good god, used by the Igorots in their granaries to guard the new harvest from envious spirits that might steal the rice.

An ancestor figure, possibly from the Amanamkai village on the As River, in the Asmat area. It is carved to contain the spirit of the ancestor after death, with the pose usually in a fetal position.

An ancestor figure also in fetal position, containing inlaid ivory teeth and eyes. Although purchased on Sumba, it is more typical of carvings from Lombok, Indonesia.

No Moslem house in Sumatra or Java would be without this symbolic painted woodcarving of the man and woman of the house. From central Sumatra.

Stupas of a wat in ruins from Ayutthaya in the south of Thailand. These structures date back to about the mid-fourteenth century.

At the ruins of Borobudur, Java, an entranceway to a room. Borobudur is one of the most impressive monuments created by man.

Hindus fled to Bali and Lombok where they continued their religious worship, and there their sculpture thrived.

Although the great stone temples, monuments such as the Borobudur near Jogjakarta in Java, crumbled in disrepair, they are being restored presently close to their earlier greatness. Borobudur is particularly remarkable. It is a ten-tiered construction—a portrait in stone of the Mahayana Buddhist's concept of the cosmic system. It is a place for worshiping and meditating. Galleries are built in ascending order with terraces. At the highest point, the symbolical center is a closed-in stupa.* And from the base up, bas-reliefs, arranged around the terraces, depict scenes from everyday events, punishment in hell, and scenes from the lives of the other various bodhisattvas. Circular terraces symbolize salvation obtained. This memorial is one of the world's most remarkable monuments.

*A stupa is an hemispherical or cylindrical mound or tower, surmounted by a spire, that houses a relic chamber that supposedly contains an ancient material bit of Buddha or other bodhisattvas.

At Borobudur, a series of three gateways leading from one terrace to another. Borobudur was built at about A.D. 800. The entire monument represents a Mahayana Buddhist transition from the lowest state of reality at the base to the most lofty achievement of enlightenment at the top.

Stone carving from Borobudur.

One of the many niches and guardians of Borobudur.

To the people of the Asmat and other groups living in West Irian (the western part of New Guinea), memorials are equally as vital, but in contrast, much more modest in proportion and temporal. To some of the people of this area, man (and woman) is a tree. Its parts are comparable to man—leaves with head, branches with arms, trunk with body, roots with feet. But more than that, the tree provides shelter, clothing, food (leaves, insects, worms), the material for transportation—and a home for ancestor spirits. The sago tree is particularly significant and figures prominently in their ceremonies. When the tree is cut down, it is a woman. Leaves are woven into the form of a woman's skirt and placed around the tree. Then the leaves are decorated with masculine symbols. Much ritual is associated with the felling of the tree and in the preparation of the wood.

Wood-carvers are involved with this ritual, and out of ceremony and skill —using axes, adzes, chisels (made by flattening one end of large iron nails), knives, and shells (for scraping and smoothing)—emerge ancestor figures, ancestor poles, spears and paddles, shafts, canoes, and prows. The shield itself represents an ancestor, and shallow relief ornamentation carved on the front symbolizes three other close relatives. V- and S-shaped designs signify animals, birds, and insects. Little hands or fingers represent elbows and hands of ghosts.

A monolyxous war shield from the Asmat area of Irian Jaya with ghost hands carved in shallow relief.

Right
Top part of a paddle or prow ornament, possibly from the Asmat area of Irian Jaya. The spirals probably represent the curled tail of an opossum or a cross-section of a nautilus shell, both common headhunting symbols.

A finely carved hardwood paddle from Irian
Jaya, 66 inches long.

Right
Detail of the carving on the paddle. Note
that the handle terminates in a ghost hand,
as do the spiral designs when they reach the
edge of the paddle. Traces of a reddish paint
can be seen on the background.

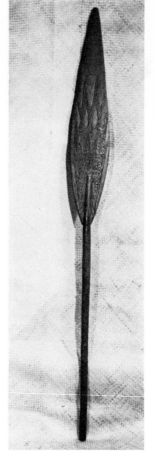

Left
Probably a slit gong beater from Irian Jaya, with
a carved figure at the top of the handle; 35
inches long.

Right
Demonic figures guard entrances and wait in
gardens, as does this wood carving from Bali.

These forms are monolyxous, inasmuch as they are carved from one piece
of wood. No parts are added. Ancestor figures, carved from the soft wood of
the sago tree, are not deemed permanent, as the memorial of Borobudur is,
but rather are often discarded in the forest so that supernatural power can
help the sago trees prosper.

Wood grain and structure suggest many types of images.

These carvers from Jasam and Pujanjan, Bali, see all kinds of demons in wood.

Their works feature bulging eyes, Rangda images, dragons, winged forms. From Jasam, Bali.

Two close-ups detailing the carving.

Skills vary among wood-carvers. And although pieces are not signed, people of the area know who produces the most satisfying results, with the greatest skill. They can even identify works by certain wood-carvers.

In Bali, gray sandstone (*paras*) monuments are found everywhere. Quarried along the riverbanks, gray sandstone is relatively soft and easy to carve. Leaves, floral forms, tendrils, and figures of all sorts prevail. Demonic figures guard entrances, others cap posts, fences, and roofs. Every upperclass household has at least one altar. There are many public temples along every route. Figures from the Hindu pantheon and mythology—Vishnu riding the Garuda, the Garuda itself, winged lions, demons, characters from the Ramayana—speak to everyone. There is a great deal of caricaturing, in a comic sense—eyes bulge, tusks protrude, gestures are exaggerated. And with every form there is a counterform. This is an essential expression of the Balinese concept of the world as one with contrasting polarities—sun and moon, day and night, gods and demons, man and woman, and so on. Rangda is female, a black form, and appears on the left side. Contrastingly, Barong is male, symbolizes day and light, and appears on the right side. Barong is a mythical "lion" who is the enemy of Rangda and fights against her on behalf of humans.

These figures are represented in stone but also in painted, carved wooden masks that are worn as part of an elaborate costume at performances.

A carving in the carving village of Jasam, Bali.

This one presides in a garden.

The tree appears to remain almost where it had fallen.

These carvings are for sale at a roadside shed in the woodcarver's village.

The sacred Barong mask, only part of a gigantic costume.

Sometimes images emerge from the bark, suggesting their own shapes, as in this mask from Bali.

Stories from the *Ramayana* and *Mahābhārata* come to life in the wayang wong mask drama. Here the Barong and Rangda are having an altercation. Barong is the protector of mankind. The widow-witch Rangda rules over evil spirits.

All the Balinese masks are hand carved, some more carefully than others. Carving and finish can vary greatly from piece to piece, even though the basic configurations of the mask are prescribed. On the left is the celestial eagle Garuda.

Wooden sculptures are also placed on altars and are carved much in the style of stone. Few wooden carved pieces are left unpainted. Use of lime in water-based colors helps protect wood from worms. There are also figures that are carved into the surfaces of tree trunks and limbs. These large pieces stand on roots that sit on the ground; branches project like many arms. These pieces are not painted and are characteristic of the wood-carving villages of Jasam and Pujanjan in Bali. Some of these tree figures are demonic, others are comic in their caricatured imagery. One part grows out of the other, often suggested by the structure of the wood.

A woodcarver from Bali refining detail of a sculpture.

A polychrome lion, *singa,* from Bali. Wings and tail are attached to the main body.

A sculpture of the celestial eagle Garuda who transported the god Vishnu.

The Dayaks carve small (and large) *hampatongs,* figures designed to provide spiritual protection against evil influences. These are sometimes strung with beads.

Two figures in detail, both in fetal positions.

Dayak ancestor figures in necklace form.

An ancient shield of the Buginese from Sengkang, Sulawesi.

Dayak shield from central Kalimantan. Raised figures are in yellow ocher against a black ground.

An antique Batak hardwood powder horn from North Sumatra. The carving is very fine and precise with head symbols integrated in the overall design; 4½ inches long.

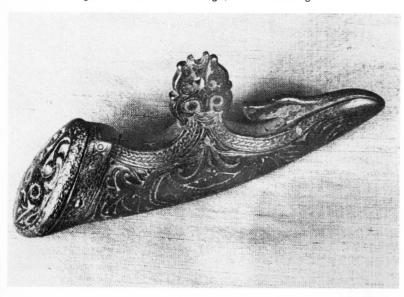

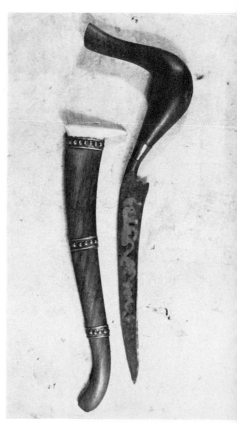

A Rencong kris in wood, brass, and ivory. The ornate blade is silver inlaid in iron. From Aceh, North Sumatra.

Opulent carving, gold leafed, from Thailand.

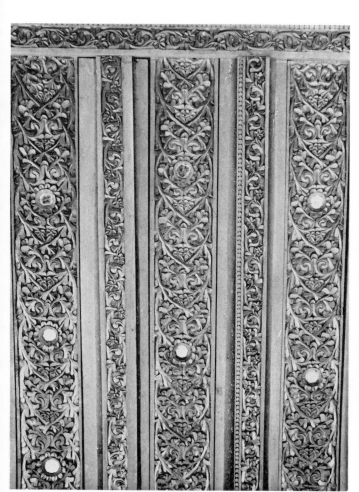

Carving on the exterior of a house in Padang, Sumatra. Mica mirror rounds are inlaid.

A carved chair from Chetyod, Chiang Mai, Thailand. Made by craftsmen of Mrs. Tantip Vichitslip's group.

A contemporary secretary with gold-leaf embellishment.

A traditional chair made by Mrs. Tantip Vichitslip's group in Thailand.

A shell inlay hardwood chest from the Philippines.
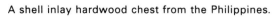

An ornately carved coffee table from Thailand.

The tabletop, covered with glass, is carved in a scene. Details are stylized in patterns that suggest texture.

Fine furniture is also carved and constructed in various parts of Southeast Asia, notably in the Philippines, in Japara—the northern coast of Java, and in Chiang Mai, Thailand. Ornamentation virtually fills the entire surface, essentially with floral forms. The effect is opulent.

Another kind of wood carving appears on the houses of the Bataks in Sumatra and the Toradjas in Sulawesi. Large homes, accommodating clans or genealogical groups, have peaked roofs bowed like a boat and traditionally covered with straw (more lately with tin), and the front and sides sport fascinating shallowly carved images, spirals, and other geometric shapes that are further defined with color.

A Karo Batak, the great house of a former king. The buffalo head on the roof is an ancient symbol of fertility.

Beautiful carvings, painted in some areas, on a Batak house in North Sumatra.

Detail of the upper gable of a Batak house.

Carved detail at the floor level of a Batak house.

A small version of a Batak house over a Christian tomb in North Sumatra.

PROCESSES

Wood

Except for wooden furniture and wooden houses, most carving is monolyxous—carved from a solid piece of wood. There are exceptions, however. In Bali, fangs, horns, wings, and other projections are often carved separately and then attached with a hide glue and small pegs.

Tools are few and simple. The adzes, large and small, other kinds of axes, chisels and gouges, knives and rasps, are used in carving. Tools are hand-powered. Paints are often ground and mixed by hand as well. The white paint used in coloring wooden masks consists of finely ground pigbone mixed with Chinese glue (a hide glue) and water. It is a white that does not quickly yellow. Other colors are essentially colors found in nature, although commercial paints are appearing here and there. Most often the number of colors are limited and used in a restrained manner.

The carving process is primarily the same everywhere. The piece is roughed out with general configurations established. Then details are refined throughout the form.

Old wooden tools—chisels, mallet and measuring string, from the Padang area of Sumatra.

One of my favorite persons from Bali, woodcarver, painter, poet, architect I. Gusti Nyoman Lempad of Ubud, Bali, who was 117 years old when this picture was taken.

Ida Bagus Ambara from Mas, Gianyor, Bali, carving a mask.

The wood is soft enough for the chisel blade to cut with just hand pressure.

A knife is used to smooth away rougher cuts of a chisel.

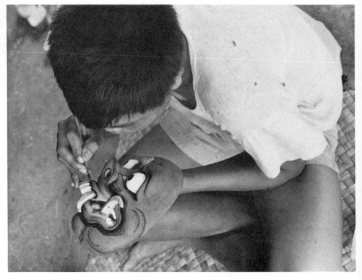

Paints are ground and mixed by hand and painted by brush. All masks are polychromed.

Rangda has a fur-trimmed, gold-leafed, leather tongue inset with mirror rounds. The hair is horsehair. Crown and ear trimming is gold-leafed leather. Earrings are red and white stuffed tubes of cotton cloth.

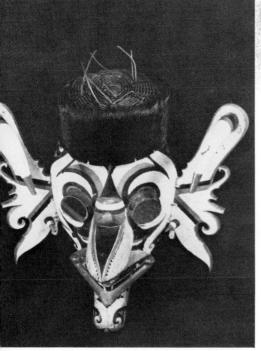

Hudok mask from Longiram district, up the Mahakam River in Kalimantan. Used in a dance to dispel demons of illness, failure, and so on. Polychromed wood with ears, horns, eyes, and teeth attached. Eyes are mirror, hat is reed and fur.

Polychromed, carved wood *topeng* mask from Awa Tengam, Java. The *topeng,* meaning mask, is a traditional mask play that commemorates historical exploits—glorified with a "bit" of fantasy, bizarre mannerisms, and a wide range of speech tones. These topeng plays are also given in Bali.

A nawe is used for carving—blocking out areas and for refining some detail, in Luzon, the Philippines.

A chess set à la Luzon Igorots.

Chess is a popular game in the Philippines. Native symbols are detailed here.

Scaled half of human size, carvers of San Luis village work in iron-wood using hand tools.

Scenes in these large sculptures are of heroic instances, local mythology, and events from the near past of Luzon.

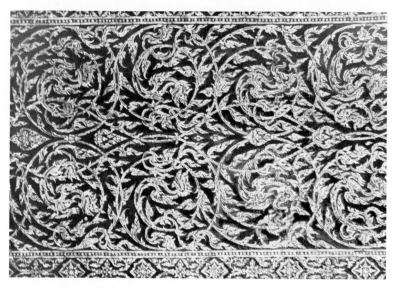

A cartoon of a Javanese woodcarving. Note the dragon form.

Intricate detail is cut with chisel (and mallet).

The headboard of a bed. Carved in Java.

A stencil pattern of a carving (Thailand).

A stop cut using mallet and chisel used to outline downward cuts in blocking out a bas-relief carving. From Thailand.

The carving stroke is always the same, whether with adzes or chisels—a stop cut and a crosscut. The *stop cut* establishes the depth of the cut at the outermost point of the cut. The *crosscut* cuts out a wedge-shaped chip, stopping at the point defined by the stop cut. This prevents too much wood from being chopped away and helps control the cutting. Chisels, gouges, and adzes are used this way. Chisels often are made by hammering out and flattening the ends of big iron nails. Sometimes knives are employed in a similar manner as chisels, although knives most often are brought in for refining operations. Small slivers of wood are cut away or almost peeled away a bit at a time. Knives replaced teeth and shells; nevertheless, shells are still used for scraping and smoothing operations. Final sanding is done by rubbing the rough surface of certain tree leaves over the wood. These leaves are as gritty and as abrasive as sandpaper.

Sometimes wood is seasoned—as in furniture making. But most often it is carved when green (freshly cut). Hardwoods such as teak, ebony, and ironwood are easier to carve in the green state. But when the wood seasons it often develops cracks and splits.

A carver from Chiang Mai completing a panel.

Details are refined with chisel and mallet, all over, a little at a time.

Various shapes of chisels are used. Note the outline of designs in the foreground that are a kind of "shorthand" indicator of the direction of leaf patterns.

After outlining the design and cutting into the background as deeply as the pattern is to go, shapes are then modeled.

A completed panel.

A rosette in repeat design inspired by the mandala.

Stone

Stone carving is carried out by cutting away small portions of the stone block using hammers and chisels. The areas to be eliminated are marked with a pencil directly on the stone. Rough cutting, as in wood, is carried out first, followed by further refinements.

In Bali, particularly in the village of Batu Bulan, lava stone is used. Since volcanoes erupt periodically in Bali, lava is easily obtained. Lava stone isn't particularly long lasting, but in the nonpolluted environment of Bali it holds up fairly well.

Stone carving in the Bali village of Batu Bulan. Lava stone is used. Designs are drawn on the stone with pencil and then cut away using hammer and chisel.

Stone carving in Bali is continuous because of the need to replace monuments.

Lava stone is relatively soft and easy to carve.

This stone monument is a guard at the entrance to a wat in Thailand.

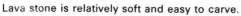

A stone giant who also "protects" a wat and its stupa, in Bangkok, Thailand.

Stone ancestor figures keep vigil at a gravesite in North Sumatra, Lake Toba area.

Carved stone steps, leading to a Batak house in Sumatra.

Old ivory-clad box from West Java. Floral details are scratched into the surface of the ivory.

The *burak,* half woman, half horse, was supposed to have transported Muhammad to heaven. This carving is one-third bone, one-third horn, and one-third wood. From Mindanao, the Philippines.

Carved ivory bracelets from Sumba. Circular decorations are pressed in with a heated, circular metal form.

Ivory, Bone, and Horn

All these materials are shaped by carving with metal tools. Ivory is the hardest of these materials. Horn, on the other hand, is relatively soft and flexible. If soaked and boiled in water, or if heated over a flame, horn can be split into thin sheets and cut or shaped. The "skeleton" of the shadow puppet is made of horn. Bone is often used, as well as shell, in the Philippines, to form inlay patterns in wooden chests.

7

POTTERY

 BACKGROUND

Clay is probably the most abundant, cheap, and easily obtainable material in the world. It is easy to prepare and does not require a great deal of technological knowledge to use. It has been one of mankind's earliest materials that was fashioned for fundamental human needs. There is a pottery tradition in at least one part of Southeast Asia that dates back more than 6,000 years. Although not the earliest known record of pottery making, the Ban Chieng potteries of northeastern Thailand are among the most significant because bronze implements were buried with pots. This tells archeologists that the Bronze Age existed here at least as early as 4500 B.C., or the fifth millennium, 1,500 years earlier than had been established.

Pottery in Southeast Asia has known several deaths and many resurgences. War often caused the loss of the art, when potters were captured and brought to another area, particularly when the rulers of Ayutthaya and Lanna Thai mounted their war elephants. They laid waste to the pottery-making towns of Sukothai and Sawankalok, three hundred miles north of today's Bangkok, Thailand, and captured their potters. These were the celadon pottery centers that rivaled the Chinese in skill and productivity. The Chinese were said to be the first to have perfected the art of celadon making 2,000 years ago in the Dragon Kilns of northern China. In A.D. 1294 the Thai King Ramkamhaeng of Sukothai brought three hundred Chinese potters from China and before long Thailand was known for its high-fired stoneware with celadon (soft green) glazes. These were then traded throughout Southeast Asia, all the way to the Philippines and Indonesia. After the war laid waste to the celadon potters' villages, celadon pottery did not see a revival until recent times. Celadon pottery is being made once again by the Thai Celadon Company near Chiang Mai in northern Thailand, closely following the ancient traditions.

Transporting large waterpots along a klong in Bangkok.

These same large water storage jugs have been used throughout Southeast Asia for centuries.

Ceramic pots such as these are essential for cooking where gourds or coconut shells would burn. These are dye pots of the T'boli from Mindanao.
Photo Courtesy: Dottie Anderson

Old pottery forms with pressed-in designs, from Luzon, the Philippines.

Teapot trimmed with brass from Java.
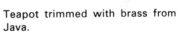

Antique celadon bowl with lotus design. From Sukothai, Thailand.

Found near Sulawesi, Indonesia, these pots, attributed to the Ming dynasty, were originally imported from China.

Another old pot imported from China, found in Sulawesi.

But this is not the only record of pottery prowess in Thailand. The potters of Ban Kahm Or, who practiced their art as mentioned earlier more than 6,000 years ago, employed techniques then that are still being practiced today (with minor variations) in parts of Thailand, the Philippines, and Indonesia, particularly in Sulawesi (Celebes). Despite this ancient tradition, the pottery art in the Philippines and Indonesia never reached the peak of expertise that it had attained in northern Thailand. The demand was not great in these places during those ages. Containers literally grew on trees there as gourds and coconuts.

Nevertheless, much beautiful pottery has been found in the Philippines and in Indonesia. Most of it, though, was imported as barter or gifts from China, Indochina, and Thailand. Pottery trade existed much earlier than 100 B.C. and was highly valued. Pieces were gradually handed down as heirlooms and used only on ceremonial occasions. After a while, some pottery was attributed to have magical power. A type of green celadon plate was reputed to change color if food placed on it had been poisoned. To the Moslem rulers, these plates had particular significance and value, and demand for them hailed all the way to the Middle East and North Africa. In some areas, people were buried with their pieces and many examples of pottery have been dug up by farmers' plows. Much was destroyed, but some pieces have ended up in the museums of Indonesia and the Philippines, with fine examples on display dating from the Han period (20 B.C.–A.D. 220) through the Ch'ing period (1644–1912).

 PROCESSES

The Paddled Pot

The potters of Ban Kham Or in Thailand, San Marchias, Luzon, the Philippines, and Campiri, Sulawesi, Indonesia, practiced pottery making without use of the potter's wheel. Instead, they flattened the clay with their hands and used wooden paddles to beat and shape the clay into jars and pots. Some used pear-shaped tools (these tools have been found at archeological sites in Ban Chieng), or smoothly polished stones on the inside, to form a male type of mold—the resistance needed for the pounding of the paddle. This process is still being practiced in these places today, virtually unchanged from the 6,000-year-old process.

Clay is blended with ashes and sand to condition it and then kneaded until the proper consistency has been achieved. It is then roughly shaped into cylindrical coils for the forming process. The thick coils of clay are pressed and patted around and around, shaping the pot by hand, until the approximate shape has been formed. If the piece is to be a very large object, the potter walks around the vessel while shaping it—quite different from using a wheel that would have enabled the potter to remain in one place.

Then, when the clay becomes almost leather hard, the "hindu," or paddle, is used for final shaping. The paddle is pounded on the outside of the vessel while a pear-shaped or mushroom-shaped form is counter-pressed on the inside, creating a resistance for the smoothing operation. The walls then grow thinner and thinner as the piece grows larger. A damp cloth is revolved around the top edge and along the surface to more finely finish the pot's lip and sides. Sometimes, as the clay becomes dryer, to a leather-hard consistency, a metal template is used to scrape the outside surface, refining the piece even more. In Sulawesi, the smaller pots are rotated in a basket on the woman's lap while she sits on the floor.

Paddle, or "hindu," and shaping stone used in Campiri, Sulawesi, for forming pots.

A mound of clay is rotated and shaped by the hand of this Buginese miss (white powder on face invites suitors).

With a stone held on the inside, the paddle is pounded against the clay . . .

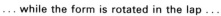

. . . while the form is rotated in the lap . . .

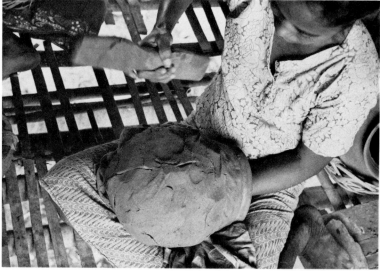

. . . and sometimes in a basket, providing a gauge for size.

Pots have dried and are stored until enough have accumulated for firing.

Two stages of pot—note that the rim has been partly refined on the pot on the right. The others are leather-hard and are in the process of drying.

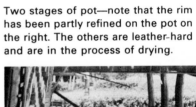

Sulawesi pots, in use for water, food, and cooking.

... pounding the clay with a paddle.

A similar paddle-formed process is employed in San Marchias, near Santo Tomas, Campanga, the Philippines. The potter moves around the pot ...

When the clay becomes leather-hard, a glass bottle is used to burnish the surface ...

... by rubbing the bottle up and down.

When completed, pots are set in the sun to dry. Sometimes the piece is finished by burnishing it, rubbing back and forth with hand pressure while using a smooth stone or a glass bottle. When the clay forms are free of water, they are placed in a pit, and a slow-burning fire, using wood or straw for fuel, is built over the stacked pots. Sometimes the "earth" kiln is covered with dirt. (This produces a reduction atmosphere, which will be discussed further on in this chapter.) Pots exposed to smoke turn black—the same as the black pots of 6,000 years ago; those not in contact with smoke turn a characteristic beige color.

Note that the lines created by burnishing become an overall texture on the large water vessel.

The pots are then fired above-ground using hay for fuel.

The result is a low-fired pot. The white clay slip provides a decorative touch. They are painted on a rotating pot before the firing process.

Wheel-Thrown Pottery

Side by side with the production of paddle-formed pottery are very sophisticated and beautifully refined shapes emerging from some form of wheel. Sometimes the wheel rotates by means of foot power, other times rotation is accomplished by revolving the wheel with a quick glance of the hand. Rags and wooden and stone tools aid the fingers in forming these shapes.

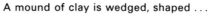

A mound of clay is wedged, shaped . . .

. . . and centered on a wheel. This wheel is hand powered.

As the wheel rotates, fingers are pressed into the soft clay mound to form a hole. Finger pressure moving toward the outside enlarges the hole.

Fingers of both hands playing against one another shape the rotating wet clay up and out, thinning the walls of the pot as the vessel grows in size.

A wet stick or a rag is used to smooth and shape the surface.

While the clay is still damp, but approaching leather-hardness, indentations are made with a stick . . .

. . . along with other textures and designs.

After firing, glazing, and refiring in a reduction atmosphere, the results are seen here. These are two celadon pots currently being produced in Thailand by the Thai Celadon Company near Chiang Mai.

Another celadon vase with small uncut gems pressed into diamond shapes, fired along with the celadon glaze.

A mound of clay, which had been centered on the wheel, is penetrated with fingers and knuckles and gradually raised up into a vessel. As the wheel rotates, fingers on the inside of the pot working in concert with fingers on the outside of the piece pull the soft malleable clay upward and/or inward or outward. If the wheel slows down, a kick or push revives the rotating action. Water is sprinkled as needed, damp rags absorb excess water and help smooth the surface or help curve the lip of the pot.

Where standardization is practiced, or where lids are made, wood or bamboo sticks act as rough measuring gauges. They also serve as finishing tools, paring away excess clay.

Glazing and decorating is a high art in Thailand. Stoneware, porcelains, and a full range of glaze effects are used. Importantly, too, stoneware-fired celadons in a reduction atmosphere are time-honored products.

Most kilns fire in an oxygen-rich atmosphere where oxygen supports combustion in the kiln chamber and oxidizes with chemicals in glaze materials to produce rich color. Iron, then, in a glaze will become amber to rust red, and copper produces green. A *reducing atmosphere* is different. When fuel such as gas, oil, or wood is burned, the carbon contained in the fuel combines with the oxygen in the atmosphere of the kiln to produce the chemical reaction of burning as in an oxidizing atmosphere. But what is different is that the supply of oxygen in a reduction kiln is limited, and the atmosphere soon fills with carbon dioxide as a result of combustion. At elevated temperatures, the free carbon and carbon monoxide by-products of the fire are starving for oxygen and will seize oxygen from any source. When the kiln atmosphere contains no further oxygen supply, the force is so powerful that oxygen from the glaze is "stolen." Iron oxides, therefore, become a celadon green. Ceramic glazes are reduced of oxygen and the color changes—iron oxide, otherwise, would have produced a tan or brown color in an oxidizing atmosphere.

A finely hand painted porcelain pot in three colors and metallic gold, from Thailand.

Indigo on a white glazed porcelain dish from Thailand fulfills an ancient tradition dating back to the first copies of Chinese pottery.

A magnificent, classic shape and pattern in indigo on white porcelain, from today's Thailand.

In sophisticated fuel-burning kilns, reduction is accomplished when the air supply is deliberately cut down and the draft in the kiln is diminished by closing the primary air ports and dampers. Unburned fuel, with no place to go, remains in the kiln and a smoky, dense atmosphere results. The degree of reduction can be controlled this way.

In more primitive kilns, reduction is a more natural occurrence, difficult to prevent. The Chinese introduced the benefits of this firing practice to the potters of Southeast Asia. They capitalized on its effects. Celadon glazes were a favorite of early Chinese and Thai potters. A frequent technique was to use a celadon glaze over a pattern that had been lightly incised in the clay. The clear glaze collected more thickly in the indentations, resulting in greater depth and modeling.

Celadons are clear glazes made in Thailand from feldspar, limestone, ash, and a small amount of red clay. The wood used to fire the kilns comes from a small jungle tree growing north of Chiang Mai. It is the ash from this tree that is supposed to help impart the typical celadon color. (If too much feldspar is used, then the glaze will craze.) Here is a typical celadon glaze formula, recommended for firing at cone 10 for a stoneware or porcelain body.

		Percentage by Weight
potassium sodium oxide	KN_aO	25
lime	C_aO	45
barium oxide	B_aO	2
zinc oxide	Z_nO	1
aluminum oxide	Al_2O_3	3
silicon dioxide	SiO_2	3.5

Only ½ of 1% of iron oxide in the glaze will result in a light green. Increasing it up to 2% will result in a darker green. All ingredients must be thoroughly ground. The kiln atmosphere must be a heavy reducing one.

Another celadon (reduction atmosphere) glaze, this one for cone 11, is:

	Percentage by Weight
feldspar	25
flint	35
whiting	20
china clay	20
iron oxide	1

Application of glazes, which are thick liquids, is usually performed by dipping the entire vessel in the glaze after a single firing (at the biscuit stage), and quickly removing it. Glaze is poured into the interior and then immediately poured out and fired up to cone 10 temperature (1260°C., or 2300°F.)

Decoration is extremely simple, sometimes with a simple line encircling the form, drawn in a light color slip (diluted clay). Other potters incise or add geometric patterns that appear near the rim, functioning as aids in gripping the piece.

In another tradition, Muang Kong, Thailand, earthenware pots wait to dry, while damp cloth over rims prevents rims from drying too soon and thereby cracking.

Terra cotta and oil are applied with a folded cloth, allowed to dry one day, before burnishing of the surface and low-firing the pieces.

The result is a glazed-surfaced pot capable of holding liquids.

These water jugs are ready for the marketplace.

Here they are filled with water, sitting outside a wat, awaiting the thirsty visitor.

When porcelainware is glazed, designs are meticulously hand-painted by brush on the surface. Since tradition has been a long time in building, most designs are classified and repeated, sometimes with some variation.

❦ CERAMIC SCULPTURES—TERRA COTTA OR EARTHENWARE

Ceramic sculptures probably were at first playful outgrowths of the more utilitarian potmaking. They soon served some religious purposes, becoming inexpensive forms that graced the peaks of thatched roofs in Bali. These closely resembled more complex carved stone embellishments for monuments and temples.

In other areas, ceramic sculptures described the life-styles and images common to lives of the people—men on horses, animals living in their villages, and so on. This is particularly true of the villagers of Kasongan, which is 10 kilometers from Jogyakarta, Java, Indonesia. Terra-cotta sculpture examples that date back for centuries miraculously survived, despite the fact that most of these forms are fired at low temperatures resulting in pieces that are quite fragile.

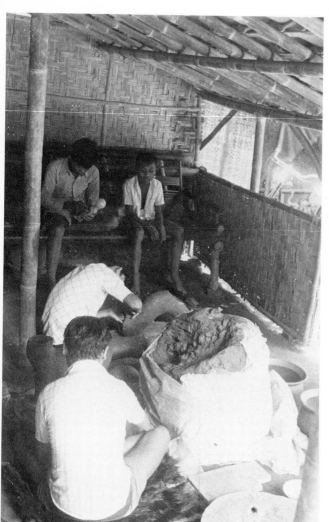

Terra-cotta clay is wedged and then shaped into hollow forms to provide the base for animal and other sculptural forms.
Photo Courtesy: Attie Suliantoro Sulaiman

Details are attached to the base and then textured with simple tools such as knives and sticks.

Fingers provide the last deft touches.
Photo Courtesy: Attie Suliantoro Sulaiman

A completed terra-cotta elephant from Kasongan, before firing in a low-fired "kiln."

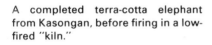

Animals both real and in fantasy are "embroidered" with clay.

This imaginary animal becomes a candleholder.

Others are meant to ornament.

Still other sculptures depict scenes from folklore and religious traditions.

Some pieces reflect aspects of the lives of the potters of Kasongan, Java.

Construction of the roof ornaments called tungkub in Pejaten, Bali, is accomplished by throwing the flowerpot-shaped base on a wheel. Ornaments are formed by pressing clay into stone, clay, or plaster molds and then attaching these in a lacy design to the basic structure.

Here in the pottery village of Kasongan, which is near Jogjakarta, pots dry out in the sun before baking.

A "kiln" is being "built." Prefired pots become an air circulating system and base for stacking the unfired pieces.
Photo Courtesy: Attie Suliantoro Sulaiman

Here some pots are being stacked . . .
Photo Courtesy: Attie Suliantoro Sulaiman

. . . into a low mound, about three to four layers high, in such a way that the fire can reach all pieces.
Photo Courtesy: Attie Suliantoro Sulaiman

Then the entire structure is covered with straw and set on fire. The baking process lasts for about an hour, at the most.

Ceramic sculpture is formed around a hollow base made by coil or slab techniques. Embellishments and appendages are superimposed by modeling shapes with assorted tools and texturing their surfaces.

Making *tungkub,* rooftop ornaments, in the pottery village of Pejaten in Bali is a timeless tradition. Here terra-cotta clay is rolled and flattened into shape . . .

. . . and pressed into a fired stoneware clay mold. Then a top companion mold is pressed onto the clay, sandwiching it into a shape.

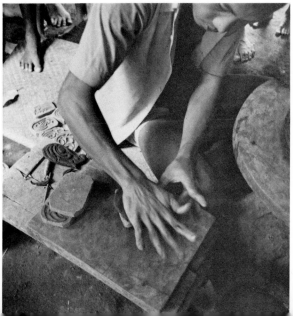

The clay is peeled out of the mold and excess is trimmed around the edge with a knife. Various mold shapes are used.

The molded parts are attached to a larger, grand design.

After firing, the completed rooftop ornaments.

A close-up view.

Another, more simple variety.

A product of Pejaten, before stacking on a rooftop . . .

. . . such as these, to become a crowning touch of beauty glorifying its straw roof.

POTTERY PROCESS IN SUMMARY

Whether pottery is shaped by paddle or wheel thrown, the pottery process in summary is shown in this flow chart sequence:

Gathering of clay

such as: china clay, porcelain, terra-cotta, ball clay

Gathering of additives to make clay body

such as: sand or flint, grog (ground up fired clay used to give body to terra-cotta for earthenware)

Optional: *Purifying clay*

Removal of impurities by soaking

Adding other ingredients including water

Conditioning clay—pounding, kneading, wedging

Shaping clay

such as: with paddles, rolling into coils, slapping into slabs, or rotating and raising form on a wheel

Form dried first at room temperature and then in the sun

(or in a slowly heated kiln)

Form fired in kiln (cone 07 or 06)

Remaining water driven off, chemical changes occur, surface becomes irreversibly hard

Result: bisque or biscuit pottery

Form porous with unglazed surface. Terra-cotta or earthenware is complete at this stage. No glazes are used

Biscuitware glazed with application of water-suspended powdered glass materials, such as celadon glaze

Glaze dries at room temperature

Form placed in kiln second time

(temperature varies with clay body and type of glaze)

Powdered glass ingredients melt and fuse to pottery body

Form completed

8

METALWORKING

 BACKGROUND

Mankind's first discovery of the use of metals was thought to have occurred when ore-bearing rocks were used as a base for a fire and people saw metals melt and then harden when cooled. From that time on, the practice of metallurgy became more and more refined. Perhaps copper was one of the earliest metals to be formed; the date is set at about 6000 to 5000 B.C. The controlled alloying of copper with tin to make bronze has been thought to have occurred about 3800 B.C.

An event of great excitement took place recently at the Non Nok Tha dig near Ban Chieng in northern Thailand. After exposing 115 prehistoric burial sites, these graves yielded a number of bronze artifacts and several small socketed ax heads along with their sandstone molds. The bronze also had a high tin content and was considered technically advanced. This seemed to indicate that these people manufactured rather than imported their bronze tools. The preliminary date was estimated at 4630 B.C.—plus or minus 520 years. This recent discovery disputes earlier theory that bronze articles were imported to the area. The controversy still rages. One group of archeologists is gathering evidence that the basic arts of civilization—agriculture, pottery, and bronze making—had begun in this part of the world. Since there is a chain of evidence indicating the progression of discovery that led to advanced bronze casting in the Near East, a group of people, earlier than the Dongsons, may have migrated to the Burma-Thailand area. All this is conjecture at this point.

Nevertheless, one of the most dominant and persisting art influences in Southeast Asia was the intervention of the Dongson culture, along with

215

Cast bronze, lost wax process, Dongson-type decoration; an antique Batak royal implement from Sumatra.

Heavy bracelet, brass, Toba Batak, northern Sumatra.

Chinese influences. The Dongson culture, merging with Eurasian influence, traveled through China to northern Vietnam certainly by 750 B.C. This was a bronze-working culture where elaborate decorations with S spirals organized in metrical repeats, along with other images, energized the plain surface of forms. This influence permeated the whole group of Pacific Islands extending beyond Indonesia to the Philippines, Melanesia, and Micronesia.

Lost-wax casting was one of the dominant processes for the making of sculptures and smaller vessels. In cire perdue, or lost wax, a wax form is encased in some kind of investment and burned out, and molten metal replaces it. Actually, metal fills the area that was once wax, leaving a new form made of metal that is revealed when the investment is removed.

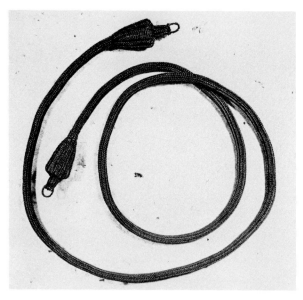

Knitted copper wire, dowry belt, Sumba.

"Kinnara"-shaped bronze oil lamp, Java.   Mythical bird, bronze, Thailand.

Sometimes large bronze plaques, vessels, and huge drums were cast in a standard bronze-founding technique of pouring molten bronze into a negative mold. After casting, the surface was sometimes chased with decoration, or design was built into the mold.

Eventually all kinds of metals were used and fashioned in a wide range of techniques, some highly sophisticated, others quite primitive, from the lost-wax process to repoussé, raising, filigree, inlaying, forging, knitting of wires, niello, and construction.

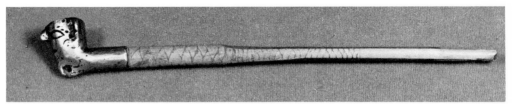

Cast bronze pipe bowl in shape of a head with bamboo stem, Bontoc, northern Luzon, the Philippines.

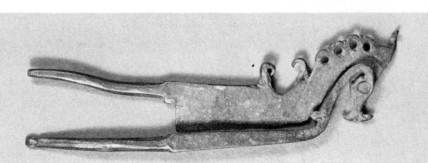

Antique iron betel nut crusher, North Sumatra.

 PROCESS

Casting

In antiquity, several basic types of molds were employed for casting sculptures and different vessels and objects. The open mold, simplest of these, was merely a depression in stone or rock containing no undercuts into which the molten metal otherwise would lock to prevent removal. Only the simplest of shapes could be cast into this kind of mold.

A second type, into which more complicated shapes could be cast repeatedly, was piece molds. These were two or more pieces that fitted tightly together, containing an opening into which the molten metal could be cast. After the mold was opened and the metal casting removed, the mold could be reused. Generally, refractory clay or metal was employed for the mold.

Another type was a piece mold used in conjunction with a false core to permit hollow castings. The core, generally made of refractory clay, filled all but a shell of the form. When the cast metal was removed, the clay core also was removed or pared down. Buddha figures were cast this way. The shape to be cast was modeled in refractory clay, and onto this model a piece mold was built up. When the piece mold was complete, the mold was removed and the original model was pared down to the size of the core, allowing a predetermined thickness for what would become the eventual walls of the sculpture. After the metal was poured, the outer mold casing was removed and sometimes the core was eliminated as well. This kind of piece mold produces flashing at the point where the mold sections join and the metal seeps through. These excess flash marks have to be removed in the final cleaning or planishing.

Cast bronze opium weight in form of mythical bird, Burma, circa 1800.

Northern Thai, cast bronze Buddha, about fifteenth century.

The fourth type, another approach to producing complex castings, is the lost-wax casting method (cire perdue). Over a core of refractory clay or wooden mold, the object is modeled in wax with the wax sheets corresponding to the thickness of the final desired metal walls.

T'boli bronze caster from Taconil, Lake Sebu, kneading and shaping wax in preparation for lost wax casting.

T'boli traditional bells, formed of wax "wire," are attached to sprues (which carry the flow of wax and are broken away later), placed in mold made of pounded rice, charcoal, and clay, before burning out in the lost wax process.

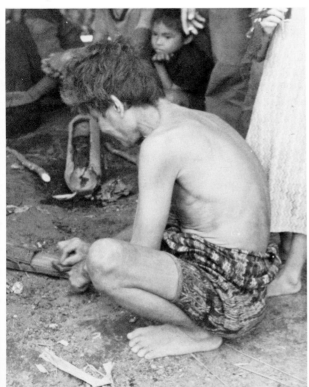

Bellows for oven where bronze is melted. Bellows of bamboo are pumped alternately and rhythmically to introduce air into fire pit area so that charcoal heat becomes more intense.

A crucible filled with molten bronze is lifted out of the fire pit . . .

. . . and poured into the mold that contains cavities left by the burned-out wax bells.

Shortly after pouring the bronze into the mold, the hot clay mold is dipped into a pot of water. Note bamboo tongs in background for handling the hot molds.

The clay crumbles away and is easily removed, releasing clusters of bronze bells.
Photos in this series courtesy: Dottie Anderson

A *lieg henumbo* was traditionally worth one horse to the T'boli of Mindanao. The primary bead is a spotted one named Mata Tahow (eye of the bird of the forest, the owl). The necklace has 28 bronze bells.

The wax is made up of beeswax, resins of trees such as almaciga in the Philippines, paraffin, and petroleum. This mixture is melted together and when it is cooled into a doughlike mixture, the wax is rolled into sheets. To retain pliability, the wax sheets are softened in warm water.

A wax formula used today in foundries is as follows:

100 parts white beeswax	50 parts petroleum jelly (petrolatum)
100 parts paraffin	(25 parts cocoa butter for cold weather)
50 parts petroleum oil	10 parts lanolin

The ingredients are melted in a double boiler and as much ammoniated mercury is added as the mixture will suspend after melting. The modeling wax will melt at approximately 180°F. Casting waxes can also be purchased ready to use. (See Supply Sources.)

T'boli lost wax castings of small figures representing aspects of their lives. The designs on alligators' backs are of Dongson influence.

Cast bronze ankle bracelet, T'boli of
Mindanao.
Photo Courtesy: Dottie Anderson

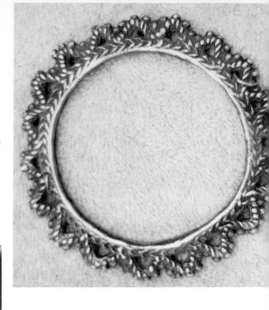

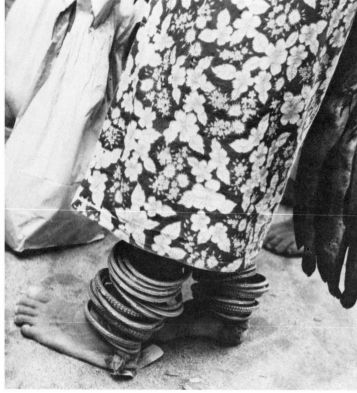

T'boli woman wearing bronze ankle
bracelets. Mindanao.
Photo Courtesy: Dottie Anderson

T'boli bronze betel nut box.
Photo Courtesy: Dottie Anderson

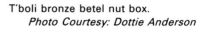

The wax is wrapped over the mold and parts are "welded" together with a hot tool resembling a soldering iron. The piece is cut away from the mold and separated into two parts. These are then fused together into a whole again. Then a mixture made of bamboo, charcoal, clay, grog (which is ground-up fired clay), and water is lined around the surface of the wax on the underside (nondecorated side) in a thicker layer than the wax itself. Then clay is filled in the remaining hollow. This provides support. Now the surface of the wax is decorated. Designs and attachments are applied at this time. Petroleum jelly is rubbed on the spot where applied designs will be, acting as an adhesive.

Powdered charcoal is then carefully pressed on over all the wax (now uncovered) with fingers until 1/2 inch thick, followed by the charcoal-clay-grog mixture in a pastelike consistency of up to 2 inches.

The whole is allowed to dry in the sun and when dry the piece is fired in an oven to burn out or melt out the wax. The oven is merely a ring of stones built around the piece with wood placed over the stones (and investment). The wood is then set on fire.

Then the bronze needs to be melted. The metal is placed in a crucible made of a clay-manure mixture. This crucible is then placed in another oven, this one equipped with bellows. The influx of oxygen greatly increases the temperature and the metal melts. Often the bellows are made of bamboo tubes connected at the base to a smaller bamboo tube leading from the bellows to a fire pit that is surrounded by large rocks. The fuel is usually straw as a starter and charcoal made from burned wood or bamboo.

When the bronze has melted in the crucible, the crucible is removed with long metal tongs equipped with a bamboo handle. The bronze is quickly poured into the mold. After a short period of cooling, the mold is broken away, while still quite hot, with a broomlike form made of coconut leaves. The porous quality of the mold makes it easy to remove. The bronze surface is then cleaned with a chisel and with hydrochloric acid until relatively clean.

The final stages involve chasing of design parts, chiseling away unwanted projections with chisel and mallet blows until the surface is free of imperfections. Inlaying of silver or copper is accomplished now, followed by further refinement in sanding, cleaning, and polishing of the bronze until it is a gleaming color. Small bronze objects can be invested and cast in a home studio quite easily with lost-wax centrifugal casting equipment sold by jewelry supply sources. Larger forms are usually brought, as wax objects, to professional casters. These pieces are usually cast and returned in an unfinished state, requiring further surface refinement.

TUGAYA, MINDANAO, BRONZE CASTING

Beeswax, almaciga (tree resin), paraffin, and petroleum are melted together in a pan.

When the wax has cooled to a doughlike consistency, it is rolled to the desired thickness. Thin sticks are used at each side to guide the "rolling pin" and set the thickness for the sheets.

A soft wooden mold (dap-dap tree) is turned to the desired shape, and a hole is drilled in the center so that, with pins inserted, the form can be rotated. Sheets of wax are soaked in lukewarm water so that the wax remains pliable until use. The sheets of wax are then wrapped over the wooden mold with edges welded together using a hot iron.

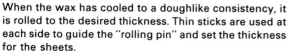

Patterns are cut into the wax.

Wherever possible, the wax is cut away in two parts, removed from the mold and welded together again. In order to maintain the shape of the now hollow wax forms, they are temporarily filled with grog (pulverized fired clay).

A close-up of the wax form showing fine details.

Another vase form ready for investment.

Charcoal made from bamboo ashes is being prepared and sifted so that it becomes a fine powder ready to be mixed for the investment of the wax.

A paste consisting of charcoal, clay, and grog is used as the first covering over the wax, completely lining the wax.

This is followed by a coarser clay and grog covering, at least one inch thick.

The loose grog is removed and a clay and grog mixture is lined on the inside. Note the spoutlike opening of the mold on the right. The others are in various stages of investment.

Molds are assembled in a circle and readied with twigs for burning out the wax.

The wax has been burned out of this mold and it is positioned now with the spout pointing up for pouring the molten bronze.

227

Here is the oven, with bamboo bellows on the right, clean-out hatch, lower left, and pit for melting crucibles of bronze, left center.

The bamboo bellows showing bamboo tubes leading from the bellows to the fire pit.

After the molten bronze has been poured, the outer covering is broken away . . .

... revealing an imperfect brass casting.

The clean-up process begins. Pieces of clay are loosened from the inside (and outside) of the container.

Cavities are cleaned out in preparation for inlaying with other metal, such as copper or silver.

Sheet copper is cut to size ...

... pounded to the proper contour ... ... and tapped in place in the cavities of the bronze.

The inlaid piece is then filed so that edges are burnished into spaces, locking the inlay into place.

Some completed *gadors* (vessels with covers) from Tugaya, Mindanao.

A fine example of a gador on a shell-inlaid wooden chest. Marawi, Mindanao.

A close-up detailing silver inlay.

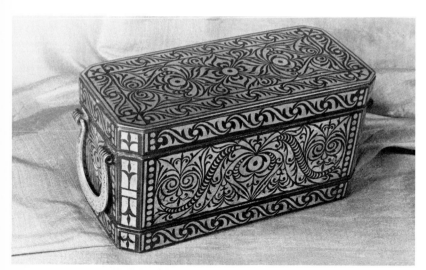

A fine example of an old cast bronze betel nut box, called a *lutu-an*. Note the heavy use of silver inlay. The interior is fitted with four hinged, lidded compartments decorated in the same manner. From Marawi, Mindanao.

Top detail of the lutuan lid. Metrical design in spiral pattern dates back to early Dongson influences.

Sinking, Raising, Repoussé, and Chasing

Raising and repoussé are found in Thailand and Java. In both places it is a fine art. Raising and repoussé are called cold-working processes. Before processes can be discussed, it is best to say a few things about the physical properties of metals such as copper, bronze, and silver. These metals are reasonably soft and can be hammered and worked relatively easily. As metal is pounded with a hammer to change its shape, it becomes increasingly hard and more brittle, until it reaches a cracking point. Physically, hammering distorts the crystalline structure of the metal, causing the crystals to part. In order to avoid this, the metal worker needs to reheat the metal to a dull red and allow it to cool. This is called annealing. A new crystalline structure results, and the metal becomes soft and malleable once again. This hammering and annealing process has to be repeated quite often. In the end, the piece is hammered and not annealed so that it remains hard and will not easily bend.

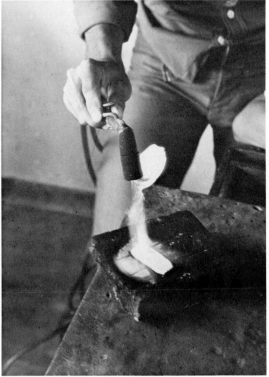

A silver bar is pounded into shape on an anvil, using a hammer.

As metal is pounded, it becomes increasingly hard and more brittle. Reheating the metal to a dull red, called annealing, reorients the molecules and the metal becomes soft and malleable again.

Once more the silver can be pounded and shaped.

When the metal ceases to respond by changing its dimensions as blows of the hammer fall, more annealing is necessary.

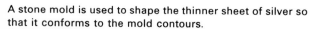

A stone mold is used to shape the thinner sheet of silver so that it conforms to the mold contours.

The annealing process continues; this time small raised pieces are annealed on a block of charcoal.

Sheet metal can be cut into shapes . . .

. . . drawn into wire and applied to background shapes and then soldered.

In order to clean the metal of oxidation scale caused by the heating process, an acid fruit called *lunakalong* by the Balinese and salt (*in foreground*) are boiled with water and the piece of fruit is placed in the hot liquid for cleansing.

Heat is applied to the liquid. The silver is kept in the boiling liquid until it looks clean.

At that point, the piece is removed from the acid bath . . .

. . . brushed with a soapy mixture, this time formed by mixing a fruit called *krerak* with water.

After rinsing in clear water, the piece is completed.

More variations on the theme of Rangda.

Some silver pendants from Celuk-Sukawati, Bali.

SHAPING METAL—SILVERSMITHING

Hammering produces different shapes. A flat piece of metal can be shaped by any one or a combination of hammering processes. *Sinking, blocking,* or *hollowing* is accomplished by hammering a piece of metal on the inside against the surface of various shaped anvils, which are often made of wood or metal. *Raising* is the opposite; hammering is done on the outside of the metal while it is held over a stake or anvil. This is the more difficult of the two processes. Hammers once were made of smooth polished stones. Now they are of various shapes and weights of steel.

To raise a flat piece of metal into a shape, metal thickness should begin at 14–18 gauge. (To determine the size of the initial disc of metal, add the depth of the form-to-be to the widest diameter-to-be.) The form is raised by holding the metal in the left hand, with the metal resting on an anvil and with hammer in the right hand, ready to strike its blow. The metal is struck and the piece is rotated constantly at every strike, with the blow administered at the same angle.

ANNEALING

When the metal begins to resist the hammer blows, it requires annealing —copper at 700°F–1200°F., bronze at 800°F–1100°F., and sterling silver at 1200°F.—or until the metal is dark red.

The metal is then placed in an annealing pan filled with lumps of pumice, or a refractory substance capable of retaining and distributing heat without melting. (Use a blue flame. A propane torch will do.) The metal usually is melted in a darkened area so that the color temperature of the metal can be gauged. The flame is moved slowly over the entire area, not at any single point, to avoid warping that might otherwise occur. (However, when doing repoussé work, it is possible to anneal one particular spot.)

After annealing, the piece is quenched immediately in a cold pickling bath or in water, while holding the object with iron tongs. (Stand back, to avoid fumes and spattering.)

After annealing, the raising procedure continues until the form takes its shape or requires further annealing.

A heavy rawhide hammer and a mushroom-shaped anvil are used to smooth blow marks for the final stage of raising.

THE REPOUSSÉ PROCESS

Decorating the surface, in Southeast Asia, is done usually by raising the design from the back or front—repoussé—so that it stands out on the front surface in relief.

In repoussé, the design is at first sketched or scratched with a sharp pointed instrument, called a *scriber,* on the surface. Then areas to be raised are worked up with tools called modeling cushions or bossing tools that are powered by hammer blows. During this process, the piece of metal, which usually has its basic shape, is resting in pitch. The pitch provides just enough resistance and give for the metal to change its shape. Alternative supports are sandbags or leather pads.

A *tracer,* which is a small chisel-shaped tool, also powered by hammer blows, is used to form indented lines following those scribed onto the surface earlier. This helps to define areas already hammered in relief or to indicate the shape to be modeled. *Chasing,* which is hammer and punch work applied to the surface, further refines these shapes.

(For those who wish to do repoussé or chasing work, pitch can be purchased already prepared, ready to be heated in a double boiler and poured to fill a hollow area.) After it is poured into the tray, or whatever will hold the form, the slightly oiled metal to be worked is placed into the pitch. Oiling aids easy removal later. (Pitch is reusable.)

Repoussé tools are not cutting tools as are engraving tools, but are shaping tools. They come in more than fifty shapes, each with a different function. The most commonly employed of these are scribers, tracers, bossing tools, modeling tools, and other specially shaped tools for specific purposes. These tools are used with repoussé or chasing hammers which have steel heads and polished faces.

After the metal has been placed in the softened pitch, deeply enough so that all surfaces to be worked are in contact with the pitch, as stated earlier, the design is scribed on the surface, then traced with a tracer. The tracer is held in the left hand, between thumb and index finger, using the third and fourth fingers to act as guides, levelers, or balancers while resting on the metal. With the tracer held perpendicular, or slightly back of the direction it is to be moving in, the top of the tracer is pounded with the hammer that is held in the right hand. With each blow, the tool is moved continuously and slowly along the line to be scribed. The result should look like an unbroken line and not appear to be jagged. After the outline has been established, modeling tools are used to emboss, or repoussé, the enclosed surfaces.

When all the work has been done on one side, the metal is reversed. To do this, the metal is lifted from the pitch by heating it with a torch and prying it away. Hot paraffin, benzine, or turpentine on a cloth, rubbed on the metal, will remove any remaining traces of pitch.

Larger silver forms are made in Thailand and Java. Here a raised silver piece is being annealed over a portable hearth. Charcoal burns in a metal dish; air introduced via a blowpipe excites the flames, raising the temperature.

Another annealing hearth, with air introduced by turning a bicycle wheel that in turn activates a bellows.

Here a ladle full of burning charcoal is brought to the silver piece and at that point is stimulated to higher temperature by blowing into a blowpipe.

Pitch is heated and applied to a silver bowl that had just been put through the annealing process.

When enough pitch is added, more pitch is poured into a supporting container and the bowl is quickly inserted.

The bowl is gently tapped into place.

Chasing work continues on the top . . .

. . . and repoussé work on the back.

Some repoussé is done on the front edge where an indentation is desired.

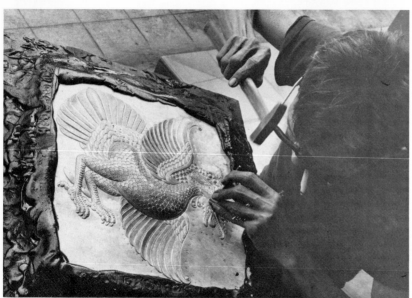

Chasing fine detail of a Garuda in silver. Made in Java.

The completed bas-relief.

If the piece requires annealing (that is, when the metal begins to resist hammer blows), it is to be done at this point, before reversing sides for further "repoussé" work. (Take care not to overheat or burn the pitch because this causes pitch to become stiff and brittle and therefore useless. Always slightly oil the surface of the metal before returning it to the pitch base.)

Chasing is continued on the front surface until the dimension of relief has been achieved. (Try to work an overall area rather than complete one part at a time. The process of reversing sides may have to be done many times before the piece is finished.)

After all chasing and repoussé work has been completed and the final dimensions have been achieved, the cleaning process begins. Filing away imperfections . . .

. . . cleaning with soap and brush . . .   . . . removing any last traces of pitch . . .

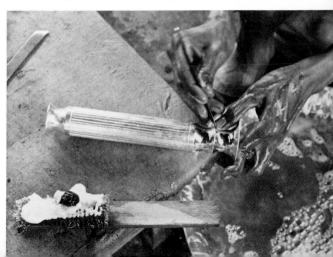

... applying rouge before buffing.

A completed silver repoussé dish and ladle from Java.

PICKLING

Pickling is the process of cleaning metal with acids to remove oxide scale that forms during annealing and other heating processes. The piece is placed in a dilute acid solution and is left in the solution until the discolorations are removed. (All pitch should be removed before placing the piece in an acid bath because pitch acts as a resist and will not dissolve in the acid.)

A usual pickling solution is ten parts of water into which one part of sulfuric acid is poured slowly (not the other way around because spattering will result). (Sparex #2 is a commercial material used as an acid substitute. It is safer, but its action is slower.) Heating the solution hastens the pickling action.

(Pickling should be accomplished in Pyrex, polyethylene, or enamel pans and the solution, which is reusable, can be stored in polyethylene or glass jars.)

When inserting or removing articles from the pickle, wooden, copper, or polyethylene tongs are utilized. The piece is then washed under cold running water before embarking on further cleaning and polishing operations.

Filigree

Filigree work, among the oldest basic forms of decorative metal, is found in many parts of Southeast Asia—the Philippines, Thailand, Malaysia, Burma, and Indonesia. Although styles vary, the process is basically the same. Annealed (soft) fine silver wire (or gold wire) is braided, twisted, and/or coiled into flat shapes. Various units are then soldered together into a whole, usually within a framework of a heavier gauge wire.

The soft wire is shaped with pointed tweezers or pliers and soldered together with hard solder. Subdivisions are also soldered and their spaces filled with coiled shapes that may be spirals, teardrops, ovals, angles, and reverse spirals. Nippers or chisels are used to cut the wire.

Solder is made by rough-filing solder sheet on a clean paper. Alum or 10 percent dry borax powder is added. This mixture is sprinkled over the entire filigree piece to be soldered. The piece is carefully placed, usually with a spatula of some kind, on a piece of asbestos, mica, or charcoal, and a torch is used to heat the metal for soldering. The piece remains under heat until the solder flows and then heat is removed immediately—or the piece is removed from the heat immediately. After each soldering, the metal must be pickled to remove oxide scale—otherwise soldering cannot be accomplished later.

Old soldered joints can be protected from heat or oxidation by using a paste of powdered rough yellow ocher or whiting and water. (Later, water aids in removal of hardened paste—to be accomplished before further pickling.)

After all parts have been soldered, the piece is cleaned with a brush and a soapy solution and then burnished (sometimes) with steel or agate burnishers.

The piece is finally thoroughly washed and dried with a soft cloth. No polishes can be used because grit gets caught in the filigree cavities and is difficult to remove.

FILIGREE WORK FROM KATOGADANG, WEST SUMATRA, BY WELISZAR

Solder is made by filing a silver bar and depositing the filings on a piece of paper.

A chunk of alum, to act as a flux, is pulverized with a hammer. The two, alum and silver, are mixed together to constitute the solder.

Fine silver wire is coiled around a needle (to begin) .

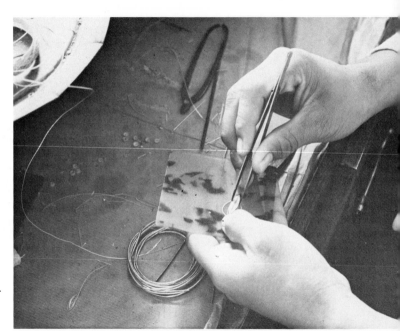

The piece is placed into the outline with pliers . . .

. . . and shaped to fit into an outer, heavier wire outline.

Then, while resting on the workbench, a piece of wood is laid over it and hit with a hammer to even out the wires and flatten the shape of the ornament.

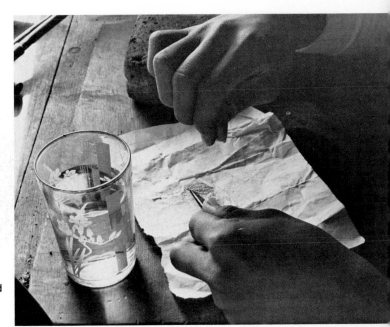

The solder mixture is sprinkled over the entire piece. . .

... and the ornament is heated until the solder flows.

This is the heating device. There is no electrical equipment for Weliszar to use. A bellows connects to a "Y" attachment above the gasoline container, feeding air to the blowtorch.

Homemade bellows.

After soldering, the piece is cleaned in acid and is then buffed with a soft cloth.

Parts are assembled into units and units become links for a silver filigree bracelet by Weliszar.

Gold-plated silver filigree belt from southern Thailand.

A close-up showing a three-dimensional variation of filigree. Parts are built over one another.

Granulation

Granulation is another classic metal-decorating process found in Southeast Asia, particularly in the Philippines, Sumatra, and in Celuk-Sukawati in Bali. Minute balls or spheres of metal, *granules,* are joined to a metal base (the same kind of metal) without use of solder.

To form the minute granules of gold or silver, a large block of charcoal is used. In Celuk-Sukawati, the tiny beads of silver or gold are made by cutting 1/8-inch squares of thin metal sheet (gold or silver) and applying heat from a torch flame about 1900°F. (they use a gasoline-fired torch charged with bellows) until the squares ball up into tiny spheres. The pieces have to be separated and not touching before being melted, else they will stick together later.

The granulation process, producing tiny spheres of metal, begins by cutting small snips of silver and separating them on a charcoal block. Heat is applied until the metal flows into a ball.

Precatory bean acts as a glue and acid. A bit of pulverized *Abrus precatorius,* which is mixed with water into a paste, is applied to the spot where the miniscule silver ball is to be attached.

The same brush is used to lift the granule and place it on the base.

A bit of low-fire silver solder is touched in place; heat is applied just to the degree that the granule will adhere to its base without losing its shape. The piece is then scrubbed clean.

Here is a gold bracelet and ring, with heavy use of granulation . . .

... as can be seen in this detail. The set is from Bali.

Spanish influence, traveling to the Philippines from another direction (other than India and China), influenced the design and process of these gold necklaces, which are filled with granulation. From Luzon.

These granules are then applied to a thoroughly cleaned surface. If the granules have oxidation scale on them, then they require cleaning in a pickling bath. Solder is not used to adhere the granules. A ground-up or pulverized inside of the precatory bean, often called the rosary pea, jequirity, or crab's-eye—*Abrus precatorius*—is used. This is a poisonous (phytotoxin) small red berry with a black end that often has been used as a bead in seed necklaces. (It grows in Florida in pods on a vine.) The seed is pulverized on a stone and mixed with a small amount of water until a paste is formed. This paste acts as a glue and coating for each granule and probably contains a metal salt. The tip of a fine brush is used to coat the granule and help position it on its base. Jewelers here use finally powdered cupric hydroxide mixed with an equal amount of gum tragacanth, with enough water to form a paste. The piece is allowed to dry and then a torch flame is applied again, slowly and evenly, while the piece rests on charcoal, until the granules adhere—but do not lose their shape. A prolonged cooling period is advised. Fine wire can also be attached this way.

This process is tricky because the granules have to be brought to the point where they would fuse to the base without melting and changing shape. The joining of gold occurs around 900°F.–1634°F. (melting of *pure* gold is at 1945°F.), so there is a bit of leeway.

To clean these pieces, the Balinese use an acid fruit called *lunakalong.* Some of this fruit, salt, and water are placed in a pot with the jewelry and brought to a boil. The piece is left in the boiling solution for a few moments until it looks clean. Then another fruit, called *krerak,* forms a soapy solution when mixed with water. A bristle brush (toothbrush), dipped in this solution, is used to buff the piece to a shine. Then it is mixed with clear water and is dried, revealing a polished surface.

Jewelers elsewhere pickle the granulated piece in a 20 percent solution of sulfuric acid, rinsing it in water, and polishing it carefully and vigorously with a brush and a soapy solution.

Silver jewelry is a sign of a woman's wealth. Heavy silver chains are made by the various hill-tribe peoples of Thailand, Burma, and Laos. Here in Pa Dua, a Yao silversmith arranges silver jump rings on a charcoal strip (made from bamboo). To the openings, he applies a mixture of flux and solder with a quill.

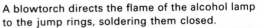

A blowtorch directs the flame of the alcohol lamp to the jump rings, soldering them closed.

One type of chain is made by squeezing each soldered link at its middle with tweezers until an hourglass shape is formed.

These flattened links are folded over one another to produce a chain.

Two necklaces growing out of the same influences. The one on the left, northern hill-tribe Thailand, and on the right from Bukittinggi, West Sumatra. Both contain various implements—nose, tooth, and ear picks, tweezers and bells.

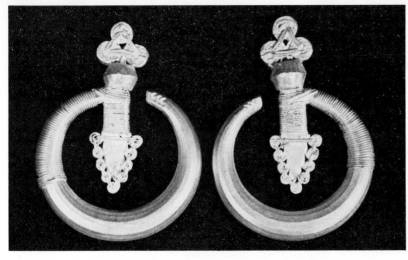

Silver earrings. Yao hill-tribe, Pa Dua, Thailand.

Silver hill-tribe necklace. Northern Thailand.

Silver hill-tribe bracelet. Northern Thailand.

Akha necklace ornament. Northern Thailand.

Akha women wearing their wealth in silver jewelry and ornaments.

Reconstructing the making of a silver link belt, à la northern Thailand hill tribe. Coils are formed with pliers . . . and are linked together.

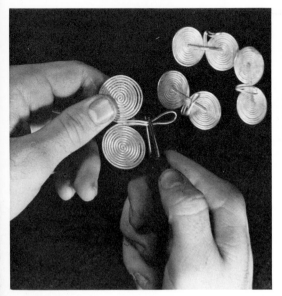 

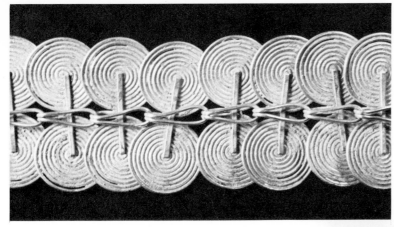

One attaches to the other . . .

. . . until a belt length has been reached. The silver repoussé buckle also hooks onto the last links of the belt. The buckle consists of two separate parts. From northern Thailand.

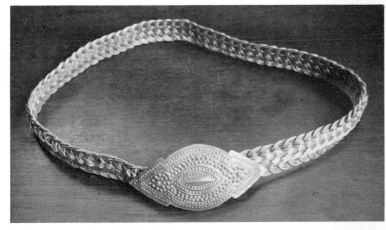

Another Thai hill-tribe belt. This time wire is plaited.

A detail.

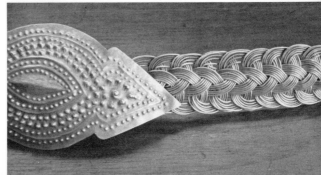

The *sari-manuk,* meaning half cock to the Maranaos of the Lake Lanao area of Mindanao. This is a totem bird, a messenger with a long history, probably stemming from India. A Maranao legend describes the sari-manuk as the bearer of love messages from the sultans to their ladyloves.

This bird comes apart for easy transportation.

A flattened version of the sari-manuk is perched on top of this silver cosmetic container from Marawi, Mindanao.

BEADS AND BODY
ORNAMENTS

 BACKGROUND

Beads have been fought for, loved for, begged for, prayed for. They have decorated humans and animals since early evidence of mankind. Beads have been thought to have strange powers as amulets, and also as a means of solving problems of bloodshedding dimensions. It is amazing to think that those tiny eyelike forms are esteemed so highly and are capable of so much power.

The Bila-an of Mindanao, the Philippines, treasure old beaded necklaces. Selling one, it is thought, would bring bad luck. The necklace has so much significance that it is used to cut the umbilical cord of a newborn child, thereby, it is believed, ensuring good health.

The finest beads of a tribe related to the Bila-an, the T'boli, are called *lieg henumbo.* The lieg consists of glass beads obtained through trading. Of these, the most valued bead is a spotted one named *mata tahow,* meaning eye of the bird of the forest—the owl. Necklaces containing these and other valuable ornaments, such as cast brass bells (making of these seen illustrated in Chapter 8), can constitute the bride price used when a child is promised in marriage at the age of two or three. This happens when a child is ill. The T'boli believe illness occurs when a child is lonely. To ensure recovery, the children are promptly promised in marriage. The mother of the boy promised in marriage crawls under a T'boli handwoven blanket where the girl child sits and she places her necklace on the girl as a symbol of the marriage promise.

Most of the earliest beads were probably traded and originally came from India and China. But old glass beads found in Borneo, in a tomb, proved to

This Bila-an woman is from a mother tribe of the T'boli. The beaded necklace she wears consists of 11 to 13 strands of beads. It is an old one and must not be sold because it has magical powers and is used to cut the umbilical cord of a newborn baby. Note the similarity of the outside necklace to the lieg henumbo.

Photo Courtesy: Dottie Anderson

The T'boli lieg henumbo also is considered to contain magical powers, particularly the spotted glass beads.

be of early Venetian manufacture. Could Marco Polo have visited there? Later, beads were made in some areas of Southeast Asia, perhaps in Sumatra, but certainly in Thailand.

Curiously, beads created of stone paste in Persia (Iran) for 6,000 years were transmitted 3,000 years later through the Indus Valley. Their blue alkaline (turquoise) frits for glazes were exported from Persia to China about that time. Interestingly, ceramic beads made a much later appearance in Europe, around A.D. 1500. Glass beads, however, were first manufactured in the fifteenth century B.C. in Egypt and in the Near East.

Compared with other kinds of ornaments, glass beads were a later-day invention. The first beads were made of hair, shells, teeth, seed pods, cloves, stones of various colors, tortoise, tusks including ivory, bones, fibers, feathers, and pearls.

T'boli necklace made of roots and tree bark. It is worn to ward off sickness and smells like ginger.

Photo Courtesy: Dottie Anderson

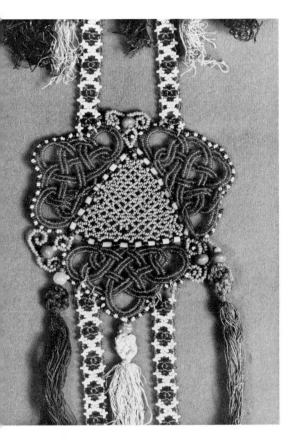

Very tiny beads, strung on wire, make up this very old ornament. It is Chinese in concept and has fine silk tassels hanging from its three central ornaments. From West Sumatra.

Beads are strung on wire and the wire is then plaited as shown in this detail. Some of the beadwork is closely knotted in a netted pattern with common threads running through the beads in order to form a design.

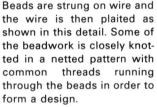

Ifugao snake backbone necklace. Northern Luzon, the Philippines.

Old clove box from Ambon, Seram, Indonesia.

Cloves are strung and sewn together as if they were beads or shells.

With two teeth per wildcat, it took extractions from thirty wildcats to make this necklace of the Ubo (Manobo Blit) people of Mindanao, the Philippines. The magical properties of the necklace protect the contents of the basket it adorns.

Photo Courtesy: Dottie Anderson

A Batak amulet from Samosir Island, Lake Toba, Sumatra. The figure is carved of bone; animal teeth form the legs. Both parts are attached with a knitted skirt. The amulet is old and was recently attached to a new necklace of seeds and beads.

Perhaps the earliest body ornaments were calendars made by tying knots in animal hair or stringing beads, to signify days, events, or other units of time. As time accumulated its traditions, the bravery of warriors, people's remarkable recoveries from adversity, or other significant events were attributed to the necklace or special body ornament worn by the lucky person. These necklaces were treasured and passed down from body to body and imitated by others. After a while that initial event was forgotten, but the import of the tooth, bead, and so on was indelibilized as an aspect of tradition.

A necklace called the *anting-anting,* made of teeth and worn by the Ifugao people of Luzon, in the Philippines, is deemed to impart good luck to the wearer. These tooth necklaces are found virtually all over Southeast Asia— and all the world, for that matter. The flat shells, called *nassa* disks in India, were thought to have magical significance. These chambered nautilus shells are still worn by some of the women of Mindanao.

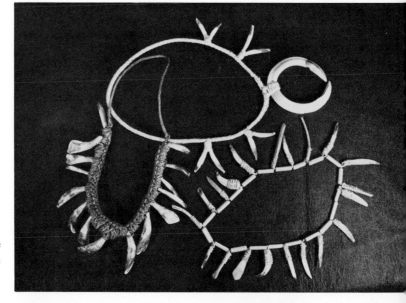

Necklaces called *anting-anting,* made of various kinds of animal teeth. Worn by the Ifugao people of Bontoc, Luzon.

Flat shells such as these were called nassa disks in India and were thought to contain magical powers. The Ubo wear these disks, the size of fifty-cent pieces, etching designs onto the chambered nautilus shells.
Photo Courtesy: Dottie Anderson

This T'boli woman, en route to fetch water in bamboo tubes wears the finest T'boli jewelry. Earrings of chambered nautilus shell, supported by fine spirals of hand-drawn brass, as thin as a fine thread. (*See below right.*)

Photo Courtesy: Dottie Anderson

The tattoo on her breast lets light into the soul. There also are tattoos on her legs to release her spirit when she dies. This T'boli woman is about 45 years old. The *lieg henumbo* necklace is worth one horse.

Photo Courtesy: Dottie Anderson

BEADMAKING

Ceramic

Ceramic beads vary, made from unbaked clay, baked clay, glazed clay, and a fine white clay called porcelain. The first clay beads were just left to dry in the sun—and were found to dissolve in water. Baked beads were waterproof.

Beads were made by rolling small bits of clay in the palm of the hand and puncturing the ball with a palm spine or fishbone or another pointed object. Another approach to making beads is to form a bead of one color of clay, then brush or coat a second thinner clay of a different color over the first, and scratching a design through the second layer to the first. (This process is called *sgraffito.*) These are the two oldest methods of making beads. The use of glazes came later. Since some minerals cause a surface to become glossy, its discovery and application was transferred to bead making. Brilliant colors resulted. A solution was found to keep glazed bits from melting and then cooling and sticking together in the kiln. To do this, beads are strung on nichrome wire before inserting in the kiln. Nichrome won't crumble when exposed to the high heat of the kiln. Porcelain beads were made later when ceramic technology advanced to a point where much higher firing of clay was possible. These beads were much finer in texture and were often glazed with brilliant colors.

Glass

The tiny, much prized glass beads that are so popular everywhere are machine-made in all sizes and colors. There have been many techniques for creating beads. Their earliest manufacture was achieved by forming a globule of heated glass around a fired clay pipe. After the glass had cooled, the bead was removed from the pipe-like clay.

Later, glass was spun into beads by heating a ball of glass and pulling it into a longer shape, which was then wound on a revolving metal bar. As the metal bar revolved, the beads became round. Color was introduced to the glass as metal oxides (copper and gold) and minerals (cobalt).

Another kind of bead reportedly was made by assembling cames of glass —long rods—melting them around a metal rod, and then removing the rod. Slices were made and individual beads were born. Rough areas were then polished by tumbling the beads. The glass tube was formed by drawing out molten glass with a blowiron, puncturing it while walking backwards and blowing gently at the same time, to maintain a cavity.

Natural Materials

Nature's objects such as shells, seeds, wood, bamboo, bones, teeth, and stones had to be perforated so that they could be strung, although some early tooth necklaces were assembled by wrapping the teeth with finely split rattan and weaving them into the necklace shape. Tusk and shell bracelets were also joined with rattan.

The use of stones—semiprecious and precious—occurred only when ways were developed to drill holes in hard materials.

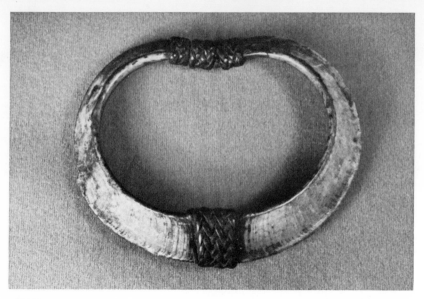

Old Ifugao bracelet consisting of two boar tusks joined with finely split rattan. From Bontoc, Luzon.

Ways of Assembling Beads and Ornaments

Beads (and beadlike materials) can be sewn on a cloth, strung, braided or plaited, woven, knotted, knitted, crocheted, appliquéd with other fabric, worked with metal wire, or set in metal.

The most common ways are to string beads or sew them on a background material. These are also the simplest means. Some kind of thread, which could be made of cotton, silk, linen, and more recently, nylon monofilament, can be used to thread beads together. After completing the threading operation, both the beginning and ending of the thread need to be joined. Knotting them together or sewing ends to a metal attachment, a catch, is the most usual solution.

Sewing beads onto another string or cloth is best described in the accompanying diagram. Overlaid stitching is used to attach beads to a backing. Usually it requires two needles and two threads.

Several threads can be braided or plaited closely or in an open effect by braiding or plaiting independent stands as if they are yarn. There generally should be no spaces left where threads cross. Beads also can be sewn to appear as if they have been plaited by threading the needle more than one time through a bead hole in order to achieve circles, diagonals, or other forms that repeat themselves.

Beads can also be strung on fine wire instead of thread. The wire can be shaped into patterns and attached to other wired sections by twisting the two wires together, or wire can be strung through common holes to create plaited or mesh effects.

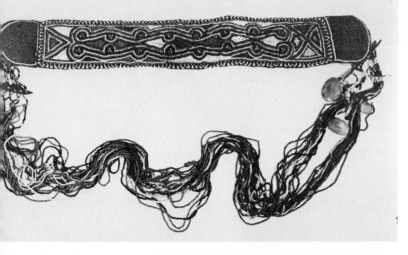

Very old Batak dance belt called *selempang raja*. From northern Sumatra.

A close-up showing that strings of beads were organized into patterns and then sewn on via couching stitches to a velvet backing. (See *c* in the diagram.)

A food offering lid, embroidered with beads. From Bali.

Another lid with beads stitched on as in *a* in the diagram.

THREE METHODS USED FOR ATTACHING BEADS TO A BACKING

a. lazy stitch

b. lockstitch

c. couching

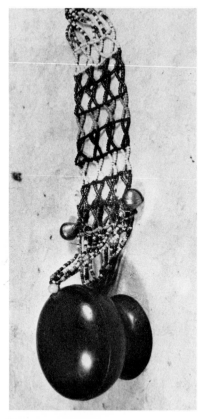

Maranao cosmetic container with lacy netted beadwork, from Marawi, Mindanao.

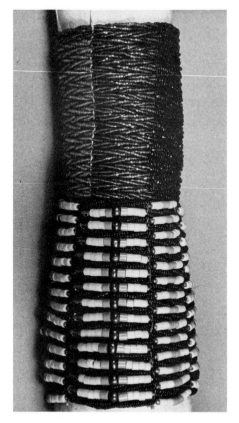

Braided and sewn "bracelet" of the Balsay, from Abra, the Philippines.

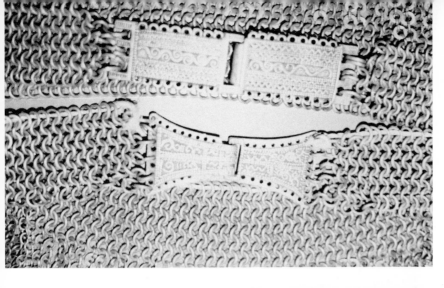

A portion of a brass belt worn by the Bila-an and the T'boli. Normally, 90 to 100 bells are attached to the brass chains dangling from a maiden's hips. The belt rings as she walks, signaling her approach to an eligible man. The buckle was cast via the lost wax process.

Photo Courtesy: Dottie Anderson

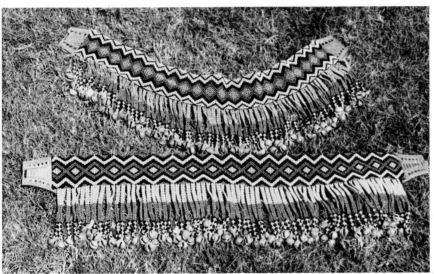

Two newer versions of the brass belt of the Bila-an and T'boli people; now in beads. These belts have only about 60 to 70 bells.

T'boli woman wearing necklaces, brass belt, and *singkil* on her legs. Twelve ankle bracelets on each leg with a ball bearing in between to make sounds.

Photo Courtesy: Dottie Anderson

T'boli hat with side pieces of netted bead-work.

Photo Courtesy: Dottie Anderson

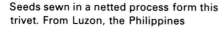

Seeds sewn in a netted process form this trivet. From Luzon, the Philippines

Generally when working with fine holed beads or beadlike materials, #9–12 needles are suitable—#12 for very tiny glass beads (seed beads). If the needle holes are very fine, as they should be, a needle threader is useful. Double silk sewing thread, waxed dental floss, nylon, or thin D.M.C. #100 crochet yarn is excellent. When weaving with beads, D.M.C. #100 is preferred for the warp and silk or nylon for the weft.

It is also possible to work with beads without employing a needle by coating the thread end with clear nail polish, or dipping the thread in melted wax. Running the thread through a block of beeswax is a good idea. It forestalls wear of the threads. Nylon monofilament generally does not require use of a needle because the nylon is stiff and smooth enough to be pushed through a hole.

When weaving beads, there should be an extra warp thread. For example, if the piece is ten beads wide, there should be eleven warp threads because each bead sits between two warp threads. Therefore, a warp thread becomes the outside boundary or selvage. It is this outside warp thread that the weft thread, used both to string and weave the beads under and over the warp, loops around, creating a selvage. For a further description, please see diagram.

BEAD WEAVING

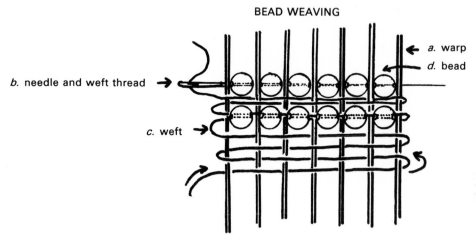

Sometimes the weft thread is woven between rows of beads, but this is not necessary. (All weaving is much more tightly compacted than this enlarged and opened diagram suggests.)

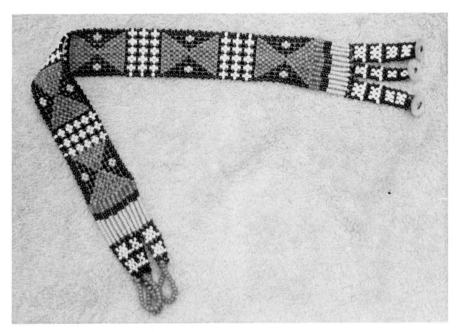

Woven ornament, Mindanao, the Philippines.

Both of these weavings, used on the elaborate marriage bed canopy of the Maranao, came from the Lake Lanao area. The weaving on the left, however, is about fifty years old and much more finely and closely woven than the recent one on the right.

 ABOUT ORNAMENTS

Ornaments range from embellishment of hair and body to attached decorations for valued personal objects such as cosmetic containers, sword sheaths, walls, baskets, and so on. Frequently, ornaments are thought to have a ritual significance, namely to represent man's most beautiful attainment in order to please the gods. Other times, as with amulets, good luck resides in the piece as a spirit, an invisible observer and dispenser of good favor. Its value more often is attributed to what a form is—what previous "life" it led rather than its rarity as one would think of a diamond or another precious gem. A valued piece is one that a person would not part with as an exchange for another object or for currency. Its value transcends material worth.

Two netted and strung bead necklaces of the T'boli.

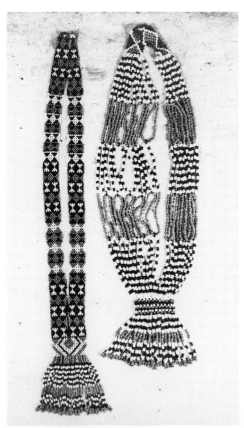

The necklaces go to market.
Photo Courtesy: Dottie Anderson

T'boli horsehair, brass, and bead earrings.

T'boli horsehair, brass, and bead necklace.

Akha woman wearing bead and silver adorned hat. Northern Thailand.

The blouse worn by this T'boli woman was embroidered with white beads on an Indianhead cotton.
Photo Courtesy: Dottie Anderson

This T'boli girl's ears were pierced seven times for these brass loop earrings. One set has a beaded attachment.
Photo Courtesy: Dottie Anderson

Old Chinese coins are used to construct sculptures and temple ornaments—offerings of the merchants and business people of Bali. Here coins are strung or stitched with cord, one to the other.

Each flat unit is built into a plane, overlapping as it aggregates into a form.

Two Balinese statues with carved wooden heads, crowns, hands, horns, feet, and bases. Holes in the wood permit attachment of coins to these appendages.

Some coin-and-bead Balinese temple ornaments. Mirrors reflect and attract the spirits.

Ornaments and offerings adorn an altar in celebration of a particular event. From Bali.

10

RITUAL EXPRESSED
IN PAINTING, PAPER,
AND PARCHMENT

 ## MASKS: DANCE-DRAMA

Whether active or passive, participation in ritual through puppet shows, dramas, dances, and paintings serves as an exorcise of evil spirits. Through these vehicles it is thought one can make contact with the spiritual world. The Balinese masks of the Barong and Rangda, as seen in Chapter 6, embody a spiritual significance because of their relation to the forces of magic and their commensurate powers to exorcise evil spirits. Purification ceremonies prior to carving the masks by only certain carvers, and prayer before performances, help maintain this special power. Because the Rangda mask is capable of emitting dangerous vibrations, it is kept covered with a white cloth, which is removed only before being placed on the performer's head. Certain Rangda masks are thought to be extremely *sakti* (magical, powerful) and are brought out only for special occasions.

Other headpieces and masks, constructed of papier-mâché, gold leaf, and rhinestones, are representative of power and are used to crown the dancer symbolically. In Burma and Thailand, court performances gradually lost religious content and have come to be enjoyed as a folk art. The stories from the *Ramayana* (Story of Rama) and the *Mahābhārata* (Great War) form the background for many Thai, Burmese, and Indonesian dance-dramas. Interestingly, these Hindu epics have survived even in areas that are now Muslim, such as in Java. As heroic tales, they can aptly be compared to the *Iliad* and the *Odyssey*. Their influence prevails as widely in Southeast Asia as Greek mythology does in Western art.

Prayer is part of the ritual before every performance and for every occasion in Bali. Here, a priest is performing a purification rite with holy water, giving offerings, and burning incense.

A circle of light around a torch becomes the stage for the Ketjak (monkey dance) performance in Bali. One hundred and fifty men provide a counterplay of sounds in a thunderous chorus that is occasioned by individual cries. All their concerted motions are meant to drive away evil, as the dance-drama unfolds another episode of Rama and his monkey allies.

The traditions of these dance-dramas date back more than a thousand years. During the T'ang dynasty in China, a troupe of Burmese dancers and musicians had visited what was at that time the cultural capital of the world, the imperial court of Ch'ang-an, and entertained the emperor. In describing the occasion, the poet Po Chü-i wrote:

> "At one blow from the copper gong,
>   their painted limbs leap,
> Pearl streams glitter as they twist,
>   as though stars are shaken from the sky."

Over the centuries, the music and dance steps in celebration of ritual have become ritualized. There are at least sixty-seven separate gestures of the hands, thirty-six glances, nine eyeball movements, seven eyebrow movements, and when going down the anatomy from neck to toes, many hundreds of combinations—each symbolizing a particular emotion or "idea." In Java and Thailand, the dancer's face is immobile and masklike; in Bali the dancer's eyes move dramatically, in Burma the dancer's face may smile or portray emotions more expressively or openly. All throughout Southeast Asia there are regional differences, but the dance-drama nonverbal vocabulary is more similar than it is different.

PAPIER-MÂCHÉ MASKMAKING

Papermaking in Borsang, near Chiang Mai, Thailand. Mulberry leaves are mixed with water and pounded into a mush.

Then, mixed again with water, the solution is deposited on portable screens by dipping the screen into a vat and lifting it out. The water drains away, trapping its web of paper. Here the screen, covered with paper, is drying in the sun.

When dry, the paper is carefully peeled away.

This handmade paper becomes the substance of these papier-mâché dance masks. After the papier-mâché (paper and glue mixture) has been smoothly applied to a mold in several layers, the piece is allowed to dry. The piece is sanded smooth; coated with gesso (*lower left*); sanded again; painted with a background coating of lacquer (*upper left*); and then painted in the various symbolic colors and patterns.

Elaborate gold and rhinestone encrusted headpieces are also made in very much the same manner as the mask.

The demon Dasagiri. From Thailand (and Burma).

Another version of Dasagiri.

 SHADOW PLAY

The shadow play employing *wayang kulit* or *wagang purwa* (depending upon where it is performed) can also be seen throughout much of Southeast Asia from Thailand, where it is called *len nang,* throughout Malaysia, *wayang kulit* there, to Java and Bali. It is considered a universal art not only because of its popularity but because puppet play entails the art of making the puppets, dancing, music, literature, and drama, providing a total visual-auditory experience for the viewer.

The origin of the various wayang performances is said to date back to the time when the Javanese were still animistic in worship. The puppet or shadow play was a way for the people to hold counsel with ancestors. In effect, even after the ruling elders were deceased, their descendents still consulted them through the spirit of the puppets, particularly in time of difficulties or for special occasions. No doubt the earliest shadow play came from India, where it is known as *chaya-nataka,* and disseminated both west to Turkey (called *karagos* there) and north and southeast to China (*ying-hi*), thence to Southeast Asia.

Shadow-puppet-making (*Narayana pan*) in Songkhla, Thailand. The tools are on hand—punch, hammer, knife, and buffalo parchment.

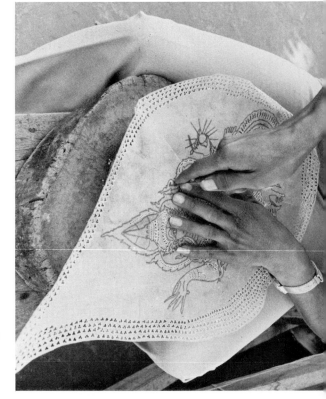

Lacy details are cut out. A penciled outline guides the puppet-maker.

Standard shapes are punched out.

Buffalo parchment at the top, un-painted figure on the left, and painted in black, as is the custom in Thailand, on the right.

Two more of a cast of many Thai shadow figures.

The mythical lion. The lacy black lines are cast as shadows against a screen.

The original *wayang kulits* were parchment portraits of deceased ancestors and, in the ritual of the play, these silhouettes functioned as receptacles for their spirits. The medium, or conductor, animated the respective images and conveyed their messages through his lips.

When the Hindus came to Java in the eighth century they brought the *Ramayana* and the *Mahābhārata* epics with them and incorporated these into the wayang. The original animistic function of the puppet integrated into the symbols of these epics.

The impact of the Hindhu epics was such that people built up an image of the characters and patterned themselves on those good traits and virtues. Supposedly, in the *Ramayana,* Sita is the ideal of womanhood, just as Rama and Laksmana are the ideal heroes. With the *Mahābhārata,* the most evident figures are Yudhisthira, Bhima, and Arjuna. Yudhisthira, the eldest of the Pandavas, is the most virtuous, but his piety does not allow him to achieve great and noble deeds though he is not inferior to the others in valor. Charity, magnanimity, and meekness are his characteristic qualities, and he pursues his course with more deliberation than his brothers—a submissive and modest attitude much admired by Javanese striving for a noble end. Bhima is the valiant knight, a man of a certain rough quality who does not fear to speak his mind freely, maintaining his point of view emphatically against all comers, particularly if one of them, in his opinion, is mistaken. Honest and courageous, of firm resolution and staunch character, he is ever ready to stake his life to defend a person or a noble cause. Arjuna is a chivalrous hero with considerate manners and stands in some respects midway between his two elder brothers. In many of the stories he appears as the darling of the fair sex rather than a suitor; women thrust their favors upon him without his seeking them. In the whole series, many unknown daughters and sons come to see him from faraway areas where he had passed through and had loved in passing.

These characters are perceptibly different and this is well brought out in the relevant wayang figures, a whole cast of puppets that differ considerably from one another. The names of the Punakawans, or humorous servants, have not been borrowed from Hindu or Indian literature but are Old Javanese, and everything points to the fact that we have here the survival of the ancient ancestor cult and an indigenous art. With the epics, the wayang kulit has satisfied a deep emotional need in the Javanese. For them, it is not just a show but represents an abstract world in which ideas become figures and imagination becomes reality. The performance is actually a mystical event in which the invisible becomes visible and something that cannot be adequately expressed in words becomes comprehensible. The wayang kulit has been able to maintain itself as a unique medium for conveying the eternal—a medium through which the interplay between man and the metaphysical world could be expressed.

The puppets are made from parchment, cut out and painted with gold and bright colors. A horn handle runs from the top through one of the feet, with a pointed end, making it possible to stand the figure by sticking it in a porous banana trunk. These can be rotated at the shoulder and elbow joints so the daland (conductor) can move them by means of thin horn rods that are attached to the hands of the puppets. All puppets are invariably stylized, becoming symbols to express the significance of each character.

In a performance, the stage is two-dimensional, employing a white screen that is tautly stretched on a vertical wooden frame where the wayang figures are moved about by the dalang. Over him hangs a lamp, the light from which falls on the puppets, thus throwing the shadows of the puppets distinctly into view on the screen.

From a wooden chest on the left side of the dalang, a rattle, consisting of several small metal plates, is suspended. These punctuate the performance with sound effects of the actions on the screen in concert with the stamping of his right toe. A small wooden hammer played in his left hand produces knocking sounds by tapping on the chest, and serves as inverted commas between dialogs of the various characters and a transition to the gamelan music. Thus the dalang not only moves the puppets but also speaks, with his multitoned voice modified to the tone and form of speech of each character, and in between gives descriptions and directions. In fact, he is the conductor and the narrator at the same time.

A roll of buffalo hide, and in the foreground a puppet is sketched on the hide.

A Javanese puppet-maker stamps out lacy patterns using an assortment of dies and chisels.

An expert eight-year-old paints the buffalo hide on both sides in prescribed colors.

His partner, six years old, skillfully inks in the fine line details. (You have to see it to believe it!)

Horn is being shaped over heat, before attaching to the puppet.

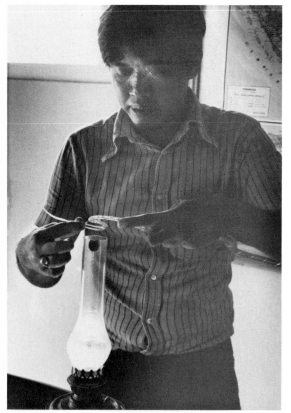

Two of many puppet figures of the wayang kulit.

A wayang kulit performance near Jogjakarta, Java. Light behind the puppet figures casts shadows on taut white screen.

On the other side of the screen, the daland (conductor), center front, manipulates the puppets, while narrating the episodes. A gamelan orchestra, on the left (and right), accompanies him. Note the size of the immediate cast of puppets. Other characters are "waiting" on the left of the daland.

Due to the immense length of the epics, the theme of a play usually covers only some episodes, but its aim is to reveal the final solution of the story with the triumph of good over evil. The wayang puppets, arranged along the banana trunk lying horizontally before the dalang, are classified also into the right and the left parties, representing the good and the bad.

An inverted heart-shaped figure, placed in the middle of the screen at the beginning of a play, is called the *gunungan,* which means mountain. It serves as a multipurpose stage prop that signifies, at different times, various aspects of the environment. Dr. Stutterheim, a Dutch scientist, saw the depiction of the Meru in it, the celestial mountain and abode of the gods and recognized

A wayang golek is a three-dimensional wood-carved puppet, dressed in appropriate costume. From Java.

These are three retired old performers of the wayang klitik. Shallow carved-wood forms, polychromed, with buffalo-hide arms.

elements of Old Asiatic culture in its ornamentations. As a stage property, when there are two gunungans, they merely serve as the curtains of the stage. They are placed on both sides of the screen to start the play and moved back to the middle when it ends. Handled separately like other puppets, the gunungans might represent wind, fire, a mountain, a palace, an obstruction on the road, or anything else not already represented in the form of a puppet.

Today, the wayang performance has become a ritual ceremony among both the Javanese and Balinese. Wayang performances are given on occasion of a marriage, after a birth (for detaching the umbilical cord), at circumcision, or for purification ceremonies—of a village or a house. The family organizes the fete and invites friends and guests from everywhere.

Wyang puppets are made of young buffalo parchment with figures cut into it with knives, chisels, and stylus in a delicate lacelike silhouette. Each detail of the character is symbolized to the smallest minutiae, using twelve different motifs for over one hundred and fifty characters in all. After cutting all interior, lacy details, the piece is rubbed smooth and painted white to serve as a ground. Characteristic colors are then painted and the rest is embellished with gold paint.

The color of the faces, which are barely human, are painted according to a predetermined symbolic color. Vishnu and his adherents are black, as well as Krishna, whereas Shiva's face is gold. Others are pink.

Wayang means "play" and *kulit* (in Malay) means "skin." These are different from the three-dimensional *wayang golek* puppets, which are carved of wood, dressed in cloth, and have arms and a head that can be manipulated. The trunk is drilled through vertically so that a rod can be manipulated to turn the head. The arms are articulated by means of long thin sticks. The heroes of wayang golek represent figures of a later period, with actions taking place during late Javanese Hinduism and dealing mainly with legends about Prince Pankji.

Another type of puppet is the *wayang klitik,* or *krutjil.* This is a flat wooden puppet, carved in shallow relief and painted, not dressed. The arms are made of parchment and can be articulated as in the wayang kulit.

This brings us around to the masked play called the *wayang topeng.* Dancers wear masks and mime their traditional stories while accompanied by the gamelan orchestra (an orchestra consisting mainly of gongs and drums). Originally, performances were given at the death rites of ancient Javanese. Wayang topeng has as many as eighty characters. Characterizations for these figures follow the conventions of the wayang kulit, or klitik, but are more expressive because of the human dimension.

The wayang is also painted on paper, cloth, or canvas to represent these figures and their stories in a graphic way. The stylizations appear as in the various wayang puppets. Chinese black ink applied as a fine line drawing with a pen and also painted by brush in gradations of gray to black is one style. Another is colorful scroll paintings. There are two kinds—the *ider-iders,* which are five- to six-yard-long strips of cloth, twelve to fifteen inches wide, that are hung under eaves for festivities; or *langses,* which are large, painted canvases functioning as wall hangings or as curtains.

Wayang topeng employs masked performers. Here is the good Barong, entering the stage.

The gamelan orchestra accompanies this performance. From Bali.

A fine line drawing on cloth of wayang scenes.

These langses are painted in lime-based watercolors. The artist depicts scenes from epic stories in a conventionalized way, using the symbols of the wayang and showing faces, most of them in two-thirds view. In order to separate different scenes on the same canvas, episodes are mounted on mountain ranges, separated by symbolic flames or by ornamental walls. The entire surface is covered in a decorative way with cloud symbols, grass, or water symbols filling in every available space. There is sometimes an attempt to represent these figures three-dimensionally with some surface modulation painted in with blended color. Everything within a wayang painting is formalized, governed by a set of rules. Even the colors are limited to five tones of red, blue, brown, yellow, a light ocher (for flesh), white and black. Wayang paintings are produced in workshops where the master painter outlines the figures and the assistants paint in details and colors.

A painter at work, painting the famous Balinese calendar. He uses lime-water colors.

Another type of painting in Bali grew out of a revival of painting in the 1930s. Before that, painting diminished because artists had received few commissions for their work. New materials were introduced—paper, ink, watercolor, and tempera, and a foreign idea—the picture frame—helped inspire a new interpretation of the painter's art. The mythical characters of the wayang turned into more human looking forms that recalled the everyday experiences of the artist's life—scenes from the marketplace, temple, festivals, and so on. Painting in Bali gained an independence from traditional form, but still lives within a new set of rules. Strangely, perspective is flattened out, raised on the picture plane as if built, one area over the other, so that the effect is two-dimensional, like the wayang langses, although figures are modeled slightly. Broad vistas and projections into the picture plane do not exist. Movement is bottom to top or from one edge to the other. Similar to the wayang langses, surfaces are crowded with forms, often encased in vegetation and tropical forests that are sometimes inhabited by strange animals. Whereas the langses are painted in Klungkung, much of this newer painting activity goes on in the villages of Ubud and Batuan, south of Ubud, Bali.

A *langses* is a large painted canvas featuring conventionalized scenes from epic stories.

An old langses from Klungkung, Bali.

In order to separate different scenes on the same canvas, episodes are mounted on mountain ranges and separated by symbolic flames. From Klungkung, Bali.

Everything within the langses is formalized, governed by a set of rules.

Departing somewhat from the tradition of the langses are contemporary paintings,
framed Western style, that depict scenes from the life and mythology of the Balinese.
This is a painting by W. J. Radjin of Batuan, Bali.

A primitive painting, artist unknown, from Bali.

Another contemporary painting, painted in the subdued colors of the 1950s, artist unknown. Most of the paintings today are painted in harsh, strident colors.

Painted by W. J. Radjin of Batuan, Bali, using variations of black and white Chinese inks.

"WE HAVE NO ART. WE DO EVERYTHING AS WELL AS WE CAN."

The Balinese language has no word for "art" and "artist." To the Balinese, art is not a category; it is a way of life. Therefore, there is no need for those definitions. Everywhere, in palaces, temples, and homes, art has been a central vehicle. People are expected to surround themselves with things of beauty. A prince, who once was a model for behavior, was expected to be able to paint a picture, carve, play a musical instrument, dance, and sing. Since few of these superhumans existed, it had been up to the prince to support actors, artists, and musicians as part of his court. People looked to their aristocracy as models of behavior and would emulate them. Thus, any farmer, shopkeeper, or coolie could become as fine an artist as the aristocrat.

In Bali, the arts still endure. There is no separation between art and ritual. People pour all their talents into preparation for these ceremonial occasions. It is a collective obligation to make things beautiful, to arrange beautiful offerings. To create beauty had been considered to be a service to society and to religion and was done gratis as a supplement to some other job.

There is a new art that has emerged. It is a self-conscious "art" developed for commerce with strangers. Much art is now created to sell—as well as, formerly, for servicing a life-style. There has been a minimum of corruption of the arts in Bali because of the significance and continuing meaning of Hinduism for the Balinese, resulting in a maintenance of culture. The painter does not paint from nature; he knows it and can bring to the canvas its essence, from a Balinese viewpoint. No matter how realistic the portrayal, a Balinese work of art is charged with cosmic and magical influences.

Styles and traditions are in flux. In the past, the Balinese absorbed aspects of Indian, Chinese, and Javanese culture. Now they are exposed to products of Western technology. I hope that the Balinese will maintain their traditional integrity and not sacrifice the quality of their work in order to appeal to the foreign marketplaces of technologically oriented people. So many of their contemporaries have lost their art in much of Southeast Asia. The consumer cult is taking hold. Where people once had so very much to be proud of, the replacements for their artistic efforts are nothing more than assembly-line copies of copies, common denominator products of machines.

A Balinese temple offering, blending some of the beautiful old, with some of the not-so-beautiful new—basins from Hong Kong.

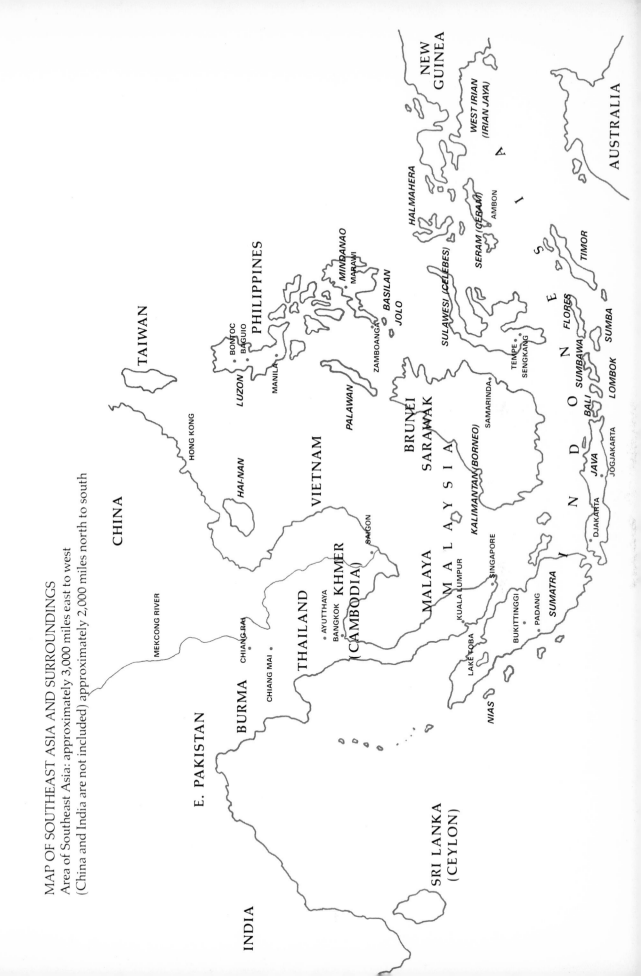

MAP OF SOUTHEAST ASIA AND SURROUNDINGS
Area of Southeast Asia: approximately 3,000 miles east to west
(China and India are not included) approximately 2,000 miles north to south

BIBLIOGRAPHY

AUSTIN, ROBERT; LEVY, DANA; and UEDA, KOICHIRO. *Bamboo.* New York and Tokyo: John Weatherhill Inc., 1972.

BARTON, R. F. *The Kabingos, Their Institutions and Custom Law.* Chicago: The University of Chicago Press, 1949.

Batik Designs. Jogjakarta, Indonesia: Batik and Handicraft Research Institute, 1971.

Batik Manual. Jogyakarta, Indonesia: Batik Research Institute, 1973.

BENEDICT, LAURA WATSON. "A Study of Bagobo Ceremonial Magic Myth." New York Academy of Sciences, vol. 25, May 15, 1916.

BIRRELL, VERLA. *The Textile Arts.* New York: Harper & Brothers, 1959.

BLACK, MARY E. *Key to Weaving.* Milwaukee: The Bruce Publishing Co., 1948.

BOWIE, THEODORE, ed. *The Arts of Thailand.* Bloomington, Ind.: University of Indiana Press, 1960.

BUTLER, JACQUELINE. *Yao Design.* Bangkok: The Siam Society, 1970.

CHATTERJI, BIJAN RAJ. *Indian Cultural Influence in Cambodia.* Calcutta: University of Calcutta, 1964.

CHI-LU, CHEN. *Material Culture of the Formosan Aborigines.* Taipei: The Taiwan Museum, 1968.

COOMARASWAMY, ANANDA K. *The Arts and Crafts of India and Ceylon.* New York: The Noonday Press, 1964.

———. *Christian and Oriental Philosophy of Art.* New York: Dover Publications, 1956.

———. *History of Indian and Indonesian Art.* New York: Dover Publications, 1965.

Craft Horizons of the American Crafts Council (issue on Asia). New York, April, 1975.

Early Chinese Art and the Pacific Basin. A Photographic Exhibition. New York: Intercultural Arts Press, 1968.

EMERY, IRENE. *The Primary Structures of Fabrics.* Washington, D.C.: The Textile Museum, 1966.

ERLANDSON, IDA-MERETE, and MOOI, HETTY. *The Bead Book.* New York: Van Nostrand Reinhold Co., 1974.

ERIKSON, JOAN MOWAT. *The Universal Bead.* New York: W. W. Norton & Co., 1969.

FERSH, SEYMOUR H. *The Story of India.* Cincinnati, Ohio: McCormick-Mathers Publishing Co., Inc., 1970.

FERSH, SEYMOUR. *India and South Asia.* New York: The Macmillan Co., 1971.

HAEDEKE, HANNS-ULRICH. *Metalwork.* New York: Universe Books, 1970.

HELD, SHIRLEY E. *Weaving.* New York: Holt, Rinehart and Winston, Inc., 1973.

HIROA, TE RANGI (PETER H. BUCK). *Arts and Crafts of Hawaii, Plaiting.* Hawaii: Bishop Museum Press, 1964.

HIROA, TE RANGI (PETER H. BUCK). *Arts and Crafts of Hawaii, Twined Baskets.* Hawaii: Bishop Museum Press, 1964.

HODGES, HENRY. *Artifacts.* London: John Baker, 1971.

HOOYKAAS, J. H., BOONKAMP, VAN LEEUVEN. *Ritual Purification of a Balinese Temple.* Amsterdam: N. V. Noord-Hollandsche Uitgever Maatschappy, Nieuive Reeks, LXVIII, #4.

JOHNSTON, MEDA PARKER, and KAUFMAN, GLEN. *Design on Fabrics.* New York: Van Nostrand Reinhold Co., 1967.

JOPLING, CAROL F., ed. *Art and Aesthetics in Primitive Societies.* New York: E. P. Dutton and Co., Inc., 1971.

KATZENBERG, DINA S. *Blue Traditions.* Baltimore: The Baltimore Museum of Art, 1974.

KEESING, FELIX M. *The Ethnohistory of Northern Luzon.* Stanford, Calif.: Stanford University Press, 1962.

KLIOT, KAETHE and JULES. *Bobbin Lace.* New York: Crown Publishers, Inc., 1973.

LANGEWIS, LAURENS, and WAGNER, FRITS A. *Decorative Art in Indonesian Textiles.* Amsterdam: Uitgeverij C.P.J. Van Der Peet, 1964.

LeMay, Reginald. *Siamese Tales Old and New.* London: Noel Douglas, 1930.
———. *The Culture of South-East Asia.* London: George Allen and Unwin Ltd., 1954.
———. *The Concise History of Buddhist Art in Siam.* Cambridge: Cambridge University Press, 1930.
Lévi-Strauss, Claude. *The Savage Mind.* Chicago: The University of Chicago Press, 1973.
Lommel, Andreas. *Prehistoric and Primitive Man.* London: Paul Hamlyn, 1966.
Moerdowo, Dr. R. *Ceremonies in Bali.* Jakarta: Bhratara, 1973.
Munsterberg, Hugo. *Art of India and Southeast Asia.* New York: Harry N. Abrams, Inc., 1970.
Museum of Modern Art. *Textiles and Ornaments of India.* New York: The Museum of Modern Art, 1956.
Otten, Charlotte M., ed. *Anthropology and Art.* New York: The Natural History Press, 1971.
Passadore, Wanda. *The Needlework Book.* New York: Simon & Schuster, 1971.
Paz, Octavio, and World Crafts Council. *In Praise of Hands.* Toronto: McClelland & Stewart Ltd., 1974.
Pospisil, Leopold. *The Kapauk Papuans of West New Guinea.* New York: Holt, Rinehart & Winston.
Postma, Antoon. *Treasure of a Minority.* Manila: Arnoldus Press, Inc., 1972.
Rajadhon, Phya Anuman. *Thailand Culture Series 1–17.* Bangkok: The National Culture Institute, 1955.
Rhodes, Daniel. *Clays and Glazes for the Potter.* Philadelphia: Chilton Co., 1959.
Rockefeller, Michael C. "The Asmat of New Guinea," from the *Journal of Michael C. Rockefeller.* New York: The Museum of Primitive Art, 1967.
Rossback, Ed. *Baskets as Textile Art.* New York: Van Nostrand Reinhold Co., 1973.
Saber, Mamitua, and Orellana, Dionisio G. *Maranao Folk Art.* Marawi City: University of the Philippines, 1973.
Severin, Timothy. *Vanishing Primitive Man.* New York: American Heritage Publishing Co., Inc., 1973.
Shin, Ba; Boisselier, Jean; and Griswold, A. B. *Papers on Asian Art and Archeology.* Ascona, Switzerland: Artibus Asial, Publishers, 1966.
Slivka, Rose, ed. *The Crafts of the Modern World.* New York: Bramhall House, 1968.
Srisavasdi, Boon Chuey. *The Hill Tribes of Siam.* Thailand: Odeon Store Ltd., 1963.
Taber, Barbara, and Anderson, Marilyn. *Backstrap Weaving.* New York: Watson-Guptill Publications, 1975.
Tidball, Harriet. *Two-Harness Textiles: The Loom-Controlled Weaves.* Santa Ana, Calif.: HTH Publishers, 1967.
Untracht, Oppi. *Metal Techniques for Craftsmen.* New York: Doubleday & Co., Inc., 1968.
Victoria & Albert Museum. *Batiks.* London: Her Majesty's Stationery Office, 1969.
Warren, Charles P. *The Batak of Palawan: A Culture in Transition.* Chicago: University of Chicago, Philippine Studies Program Research Series #3. 1964.
Wilson, Jean. *Weaving Is for Everyone.* New York: Reinhold Publishing Corp., 1967.
Wingert, Paul S. *Primitive Art.* New York: Oxford University Press, 1962.
Wood, W. A. R. *A History of Siam.* Bangkok: Chalermnit Book Shop, 1959.
Znamierowski, Nell. *Step by Step Weaving.* New York: Golden Press, 1967.

SUPPLY SOURCES

BAMBOO

Bamboo & Rattan Works
901 Jefferson St.
Hoboken, N.J. 07030
bamboo—all sizes

The Otto Gerdau Co.
82 Wall St.
New York, N.Y. 10005
narrow diameter bamboo and bamboo board

BASKETMAKING

Cane & Basket Supply Co.
1283 S. Cochran Ave.
Los Angeles, Calif. 90019
basketry supplies

Creative Handweavers
P.O. Box 26480
Los Angeles, Calif. 90026
basketry supplies

Lejeune Swisstraw
Lejeune, Inc.
Sunnyvale, Calif. 94086
artificial raffia

Naturalcraft
2199 Bancroft Way
Berkeley, Calif. 94704
basketry supplies

Savin Handcrafts
P.O. Box 4251
Hamden, Conn. 06514
grasses, reeds, cane, rush, etc.

BATIK

Aiko's Art Materials
714 N. Wabash Ave.
Chicago, Ill. 60611
batik materials and dyes

Aljo Manufacturing Co., Inc.
116 Prince St.
New York, N.Y. 10012
batik mat and dyes

Dharma Trading Co.
1952 University Ave.
Berkeley, Calif. 94701
batik mat and dyes

Frank B. Ross Co., Inc.
6 Ash St.
Jersey City, N.J. 07304
waxes

Screen Process Supplies
1199 East 12th St.
Oakland, Calif. 94606
batik mat and dyes

Straw Into Gold
5509 College Ave.
P.O. Box 2904
Oakland, Calif. 94618
batik supplies

Yellow Springs Strings, Inc.
P.O. Box 107
Route 68, Goes Station
Yellow Springs, Ohio 45387
batik materials

BEADS

Bead Game
505 N. Fairfax Ave.
Los Angeles, Calif. 90036
beads and beadworking supplies

Clyde N. Jund
460 Lakeview Ave.
Winter Park, Fla. 32789
shells

Many Feathers Trading Co.
1855 East 15th St.
Tulsa, Okla. 74101
beads and beadworking supplies

Northeast Bead Trading Co.
12 Depot St.
Kennebunk, Maine 04043
beads and beadworking supplies

Straw Into Gold
5509 College Ave.
P.O. Box 2904
Oakland, Calif. 94618
beads

Taiwan Variety and Novelty Supplies
2 Alley 11, Lane 174
Sec. 2, Pa-Teh Rd.
Taipei, Taiwan
mother-of-pearl, shells, beads, etc.

Walco Products, Co.
1200 Zerega Ave.
Bronx, N.Y. 10462
beads and looms

Winona Trading Post
P.O. Box 324
Santa Fe, N.M. 87501
beads, shells, abalone

BUFFALO LEATHER

For directory, write:

Tanners' Council of America
411 Fifth Ave.
New York, N.Y. 10016

Mac Leather Co.
424 Broome St.
New York, N.Y. 10013

CLAY

American Art Clay Co.
Indianapolis, Ind. 46200
*Mexican pottery clay—self-hardening tools
and supplies*

House of Ceramics, Inc.
1011 N. Hollywood St.
Memphis, Tenn. 38108
complete line

Newton Pottery Supply Co.
96 Rumford Ave.
Box 96
West Newton, Mass. 02165
complete line

Standard Ceramic Supply Co.
Box 4435
Pittsburgh, Pa. 15205
complete line

Stewart Clay Co., Inc.
133 Mulberry St.
New York, N.Y. 10013
clay, tools, and supplies

Trinity Ceramic Supply Inc.
9016 Diplomacy Row
Dallas, Texas 75235
complete line

EMBROIDERY

Marribee
2904 W. Lancaster
Fort Worth, Texas
embroidery yarn and threads

Thumbelina Needlework
1685 Copenhagen Drive
Solvang, Calif. 93463
embroidery threads

GENERAL SUPPLIES

Bergen Arts and Crafts
P.O. Box 689
Salem, Mass. 01970
complete line, including beads, of arts and crafts

Dick Blick
Box 1267
Galesburg, Ill. 61401
complete line of arts and crafts material

Brookstone Co.
Peterborough, N.H. 03458
mail order suppliers of tools, wire, etc.

CCM Arts & Crafts, Inc.
9520 Baltimore Ave.
College Park, Md. 20740
complete line of arts and crafts material

Economy Arts and Crafts
47–11 Francis Lewis Blvd.
Flushing, N.Y. 11361
complete line

J. L. Hammett Co.
2393 Vauxhall Road
Union, N.J. 07083

  165 Water Street
  Lyons, N.Y. 14489

  Hammett Place
  Braintree, Mass. 02184

  U.S. Route 29 South
  Lynchburg, Va. 24502
*complete line of arts and crafts material,
plus weaving supplies and equipment*

Nasco
901 Janesville Avenue
Fort Atkinson, Wis. 53538
*complete line of arts and crafts materials
plus basketry*

Sax Arts and Crafts
207 N. Milwaukee St.
Milwaukee, Wis. 53202
*Complete line of arts and crafts materials
plus clays and ceramic supplies*

GOURD SEEDS

W. Atlee Burpee Co.
P.O. Box 6929
Philadelphia, Pa. 19132

Henry Field
Shenandoah, Iowa

Stokes Seeds, Inc.
P.O. Box 548, Main P.O.
Buffalo, N.Y. 14240

METAL WORKING

Abbey Materials Corp.
116 West 29th Street
New York, N.Y. 10001
casting and casting materials

Allcraft Tool and Supply Co., Inc.
15 West 45th Street
New York, N.Y. 10036
*complete line of wires and metalworking
materials*

Billanti Casting Company
64 West 48th Street
New York, N.Y. 10036
lost-wax casting service

Kerr Dental Manufacturing Company
6081–6095 12th Street
Detroit, Mich.
*wax wire and investment compounds and
supplies*

PAPIER-MÂCHÉ

Activa Products, Inc.
7 Front Street
San Francisco, Calif.
Celluclay instant papier-mâché

Henkel, Inc.
Teaneck, N.J. 07666
Metylan paste for papier-mâché

WEAVING

The Handweaver
460 First Street East
Sonoma, Calif. 95476
yarns, and materials for weavers

The Silver Shuttle
1301 35th Street N.W.
Washington, D.C. 20007
*assorted yarns and fibers and all kinds of
weaving materials*

Some Place
2990 Adeline Street
Berkeley, Calif. 94703
weaving materials and equipment

Straw Into Gold. See "Beads."
all kinds of yarns and materials for weavers

Yellow Springs Strings, Inc.
P.O. Box 107
Route 68, Goes Station
Yellow Springs, Ohio 45387
assorted yarns and fibers

WOOD

Buck Bros., Inc.
Millbury, Mass. 01527
wood-carving tools

Albert Constantine and Sons Inc.
2050 Eastchester Road
Bronx, N.Y. 10461
assorted woods and veneers

Craftsman Wood Service Co.
2272 South Mary Street
Chicago, Ill. 60608
assorted woods and veneers

Leichtung
187 Mayfield Road
Cleveland, Ohio 44124
wood-carving tools and benches

Sculpture Associates
114 East 25th Street
New York, N.Y. 10010
stone, wood, and tools

Sculpture Services, Inc.
9 East 19th Street
New York, N.Y. 10003
stone, wood, and tools

INDEX